Elementary

Student's Book

New Headway
English Course

Liz and John Soars

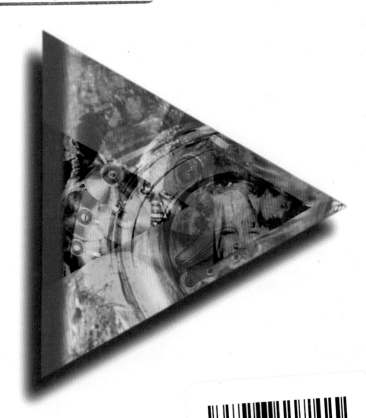

OXFORD
UNIVERSITY PRESS

CONTENTS

147652

Stop and check 1   Teacher's Book p138

1 Hello everybody!

am/is/are · my/your/his/her · Everyday objects · Numbers · Hello and goodbye

STARTER

1 Say your names.

> I'm Ali.

> I'm Tomas.

2 Stand up in alphabetical order and say your names.

> I'm Ali.

> I'm Birgit.

> I'm Tomas.

> I'm Zak.

INTRODUCTIONS
am/is/are, my/your

1 **T 1.1** Read and listen.

  A Hello. My name's Paula.
     What's your name?
  B Rosa.
  A Where are you from, Rosa?
  B I'm from Chicago.

  T 1.1 Listen and repeat.

GRAMMAR SPOT
name's = name is what's = what is I'm = I am

2 Write the conversation.

A Hello. My _____ Richard. What's _____ name?

B Kurt.

A _____ are you from, Kurt?

B _____ from Hamburg. Where _____ you from?

A _____ _____ London.

T 1.2 Listen and check.

3 Stand up! Talk to the students in the class.

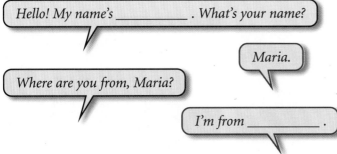

Hello! My name's _____ . What's your name?

Maria.

Where are you from, Maria?

I'm from _____ .

Countries, *his/her*

4 **T 1.3** Listen and repeat.

	● ●	● ●	● ● ●
the USA Spain France	Egypt Russia England	Brazil Japan	Mexico Germany Italy Hungary

5 Read about the people.

¡Buenos días!

This is Rafael.
He's from Mexico.

Salem ala goum!

This is Yasmina.
She's from Egypt.

Hi!

This is Max and Lisa.
They're from the USA.

6 Where are the people from? Write the countries from exercise 4.

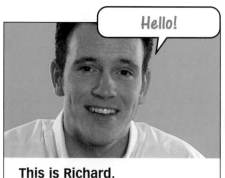

Hello!

This is Richard.
He's from England.

Konnichiwa!

This is Tomoko.
She's from Japan.

Bom dia!

This is Lena and Miguel.
_____

Buongiorno!

This is Anna.
_____

Privyet!

This is Irina.
_____

Sziasztok!

This is László and Ilona.
_____

¡Buenos días!

This is María.
_____

Guten Tag!

This is Kurt.
_____

Bonjour!

This is Pierre.
_____

7 Ask and answer questions about the people.
Use *he/his* and *she/her*.

What's his name? — Richard.

Where's he from? — England.

What's her name? — Tomoko.

Where's she from? — Japan.

GRAMMAR SPOT

Complete the table with *am*, *is*, and *are*.

I	_____	
He She It	_____	from England.
We You They	_____	

▶▶ **Grammar Reference 1.1 p124**

PRACTICE

Talking about you

1 Ask and answer questions with a partner about the students in your class.

What's his name?

Where's he from?

2 Introduce your partner to the class.

This is Kurt. He's from Hamburg in Germany.

Listening and pronunciation

3 **T 1.4** Listen and tick (✓) the sentence you hear.

1 ☐ She's from Spain.
   ☐ He's from Spain.
2 ☐ What's her name?
   ☐ What's his name?
3 ☐ They're from Brazil.
   ☐ They're in Brazil.
4 ☐ Where's she from?
   ☐ Where's he from?
5 ☐ He's a teacher in Italy.
   ☐ She's a teacher in Italy.

Check it

4 Complete the sentences with *am, is, are, his, her,* or *your*.

1 My name __is__ Anna.
2 Where _____ you from?
3 I _____ from Japan.
4 'What's _____ name?' 'My name's Tomoko.'
5 Max and Lisa _____ from Chicago.
6 This _____ my teacher. _____ name's Richard.
7 Where _____ he from?
8 This is my sister. _____ name's Emma.

Reading and writing

5 **T 1.5** Listen and read about Rafael.

My name's Rafael Ramos and I'm a doctor. I'm 30. I'm married and I have two children. I live in a house in Toluca in Mexico. I want to learn English for my job.

6 Complete the text about Yasmina.

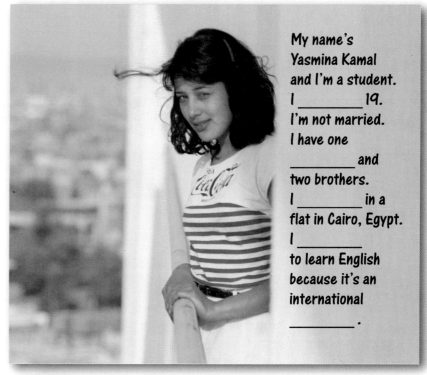

My name's Yasmina Kamal and I'm a student. I _____ 19. I'm not married. I have one _____ and two brothers. I _____ in a flat in Cairo, Egypt. I _____ to learn English because it's an international _____ .

T 1.6 Listen and check.

7 Write about you. Then read it to the class.

VOCABULARY AND PRONUNCIATION
Everyday objects

1 **T 1.7** Listen to the alphabet song. Say the alphabet as a class.

2 Look at this extract from an English/Spanish dictionary.

the word in English → the part of speech (n. = noun)

apple /ˈæpl/ n. *manzana*

the pronunciation ↗ ↖ the word in Spanish

3 Match the words and pictures.

	• •	• • •	• • •
a stamp a bag a key	a camera a ticket a postcard a letter an apple an orange	a dictionary a newspaper	a magazine

T 1.8 Listen and repeat.

4 Ask and answer questions with a partner.

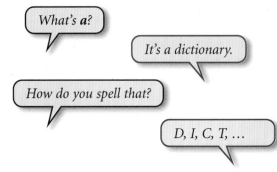

What's a?

It's a dictionary.

How do you spell that?

D, I, C, T, ...

5 Look at the words. What are *a, e, i, o,* and *u*? When is it *a*? When is it *an*?

a bag	*an* apple
a ticket	*an* orange
a letter	*an* English book

6 Look at the plural words.

two stamps   two apples   two dictionaries

Say the plurals of the other words in exercise 3.

▶▶ **Grammar Reference 1.4 and 1.5 p124**

EVERYDAY ENGLISH
Hello and goodbye

1 Say the numbers 1–20 round the class.

2 **T 1.9** Read and listen to the telephone numbers.

682 947	six eight two	nine four seven
8944 5033	eight nine *double* four	five 'oh' *double* three
020 7399 7050	'oh' two 'oh'	seven three *double* nine	seven 'oh' five 'oh'

3 **T 1.10** Listen and write the numbers you hear. Practise them.

4 Ask and answer the question with other students. Write a list.

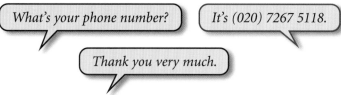

What's your phone number?

It's (020) 7267 5118.

Thank you very much.

5 Write the conversations in the correct order.

1 I'm fine, thank you. And you?
   I'm OK, thanks.
   Hello, Mary. This is Edward.
       How are you?
   Hello, extension 3442.

   A _____
   B _____
   A _____
   B _____

2 Goodbye, Bianca. Have a nice day.
   Yes, at seven in the cinema.
   Thanks, Marcus. See you this
       evening!
   Goodbye, Marcus.

   A _____
   B _____
   A _____
   B _____

3 Not bad, thanks. And you?
   Very well. How are the children?
   Hi, Flora! It's me, Leo. How are you?
   They're fine.
   Hello, 270899.

   A _____
   B _____
   A _____
   B _____
   A _____

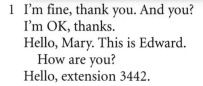

T 1.11 Listen and check.

6 Practise the conversations with other students. Practise again, using your names and numbers.

Meeting people

am/is/are – questions and negatives · Possessive 's · Family · Opposites · In a café

1 Count from 1–20 round the class.

2 Count in 10s from 10–100 round the class.
ten, twenty, thirty . . . one hundred.

3 How old are you? Ask and answer in groups.

WHO IS SHE?
Questions and negatives

1 Read Keesha Anderson's identity card.

2 Complete the questions.

1 What's __her__ surname? Anderson.
2 _____ her first name? Keesha.
3 _____ she from? London, England.
4 _____ _____ job? She's a journalist.
5 What's _____ _____ ? 42, Muswell Hill Road,
London N10 3JD.
6 _____ _____ phone 020 8863 5741.
number?
7 How old _____ _____ ? Twenty-eight.
8 Is she _____ ? No, she isn't.

T 2.1 Listen and check. Practise the questions and answers.

3 Keesha has a brother. Write questions about him. Ask your teacher and complete his card.

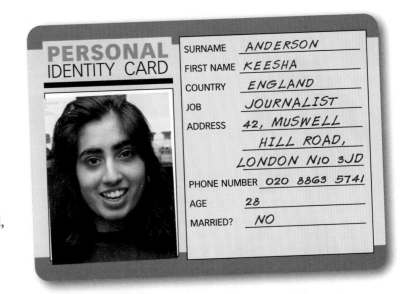

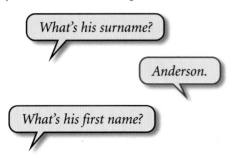

What's his surname?

Anderson.

What's his first name?

Negatives and short answers

4 [T 2.2] Read and listen. Then listen and repeat.

Is she American?

No, she isn't.

Is she French?

No, she isn't.

Is she English?

Yes, she is.

Ask and answer *Yes/No* questions about Keesha.
1 a doctor? a teacher? a journalist?
2 eighteen? twenty-one? twenty-eight?

5 Ask and answer questions about Keesha's brother.
1 Peter? Daniel? Rudi?
2 a journalist? a student? a policeman?
3 sixteen? thirty? twenty-one?

GRAMMAR SPOT

1 Complete the answers to the *Yes/No* questions.
Is Keesha English?
Yes, she _____ .
Is her surname Smith?
No, it _____ .
Are you a journalist?
No, I'm _____ .

2 Look at the negatives.
She **isn't** married.
You **aren't** English.
But: I'**m not** a teacher
✗ I amn't a teacher.

▶▶ **Grammar Reference 2.1 p125**

PRACTICE

Who is he?

1 **Student A** Look at the identity card from your teacher.
Student B Look at this identity card.

Ask and answer questions to complete the information.

RBS INTERNATIONAL **IDENTITY CARD**

SURNAME ....
FIRST NAME PATRICK
COUNTRY ....
JOB ACCOUNTANT
ADDRESS ....

PHONE NUMBER 1232 4837
AGE ....
MARRIED? YES

2 Ask and answer *Yes/No* questions about Patrick.
1 Smith? Jones? Binchey?
2 from Italy? from England? from Ireland?
3 a policeman? a teacher? an accountant?

Talking about you

3 Ask your teacher some questions.

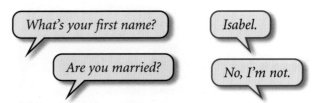

What's your first name?

Isabel.

Are you married?

No, I'm not.

4 Look at the form from your teacher.

Stand up! Ask two students *Yes/No* questions to complete the form. Answer questions about you.

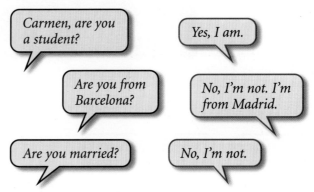

Carmen, are you a student?

Yes, I am.

Are you from Barcelona?

No, I'm not. I'm from Madrid.

Are you married?

No, I'm not.

Tell the class about one of the students.

Her name's Anna-Maria. She's a student …

PATRICK'S FAMILY
Possessive 's

1 Write these words in the correct place.

brother	father	daughter	wife	aunt	grandmother

🚹	boyfriend	husband		son		uncle	grandfather
🚺	*girlfriend*		mother		sister		

2 **T 2.3** Read about Patrick Binchey and listen. Write the names of the people in the correct place.

This is a photo of **Patrick**, his wife, and his children. His wife's name is Brenda. She's a teacher. His daughter's name is Lara. She's twenty-one and she's a nurse. His son's name is Benny. He's nineteen and he's a student. Lara's boyfriend is a nurse, too. His name is Mick.

1

2

3

4

5

3 Ask and answer questions about Patrick's family.

Who's Brenda?   *She's Patrick's wife.*

> **GRAMMAR SPOT**
>
> **1** Look at *'s*.
>   She**'s** a teacher: She's = She is.
>   His wife**'s** name: His wife's name = her name
>   's = possession.
> **2** Find other examples in the text of possessive *'s* and *'s* = is.
> ▶▶ **Grammar Reference 2.2 p125**

PRACTICE

You and your family

1 Ask your teacher questions about the people in his/her family.

> *What's your mother's name?*

> *What's your sister's name?*

2 Write the names of people in your family. Ask and answer questions with a partner.

Juan   Silvia   María   Fernando   Amelia

Ask a partner questions about his/her family.

> *Who's Juan?*

> *He's my brother.*

> *Who's Silvia?*

> *She's my aunt.
> She's my mother's sister.*

3 Make true sentences with the verb *to be*.

1 I **'m not** _____ at home.
2 We _____ in class.
3 It _____ Monday today.
4 My teacher's name _____ John.
5 My mother and father _____ at work.
6 I _____ married.
7 My grandmother _____ seventy-five years old.
8 Marcus and Carlos _____ my brothers.
9 We _____ in the coffee bar. We _____ in the classroom.

Check it

4 Tick (✓) the correct sentence.

1 ☐ I'm a doctor.
   ☐ I'm doctor.

2 ☐ I have twenty-nine years old.
   ☐ I am twenty-nine years old.

3 ☐ I no married.
   ☐ I'm not married.

4 ☐ My sister's name is Lara.
   ☐ My sisters name is Lara.

5 ☐ She married.
   ☐ She's married.

6 ☐ I'm an uncle.
   ☐ I'm a uncle.

7 ☐ I have two brother.
   ☐ I have two brothers.

8 ☐ Peter's the son of my sister.
   ☐ Peter's my sister's son.

VOCABULARY
Opposites

1 Match the adjectives with their opposites.

old	horrible
big	old
new	young
lovely	difficult
easy	cheap
hot	cold
expensive	slow
fast	small

2 Write about the pictures, using the adjectives.

1 _He's old._   _She's young._

$$2+2=4$$ $$2x^2+2x-8$$

2 _____ _____

3 _____ _____

4 _____ _____

5 _____ _____

6 _____ _____

7 _____ _____

8 _____ _____

T 2.4 Listen and check. Practise saying the sentences.

READING AND LISTENING
A letter from America

1 **T 2.5** Dorita is an English student at a school in Queens, New York City. Read and listen to her letter to Miguel, her brother in Argentina.

2 Match each photograph with part of the letter.

3 Correct the false (✗) sentences.
1 Dorita is from Argentina. ✓
2 She's in Miami. ✗ **No, she isn't. She's in New York.**
3 Dorita's happy in New York.
4 She's on holiday.
5 It's a very big class.
6 The students in her class are all from South America.
7 Annie and Marnie are both students.
8 The subway is easy to use.

4 Write the questions about Dorita's letter.

1   **Where's Dorita from?** _____ ?
   Argentina.

2 _____ ?
   Japan, Brazil, Switzerland, Poland, and Italy.

3 _____ ?
   Isabel.

4 _____ ?
   They are sisters. They live with Dorita.

5 _____ ?
   Annie's twenty and Marnie's eighteen.

6 _____ New York _____ ?
   Yes, it is.

5 **T 2.6** Listen to three conversations. Where is Dorita? Who is she with?

Writing

6 Write a letter about *your* class.

2

3

4

5

41 46th Street
Sunnyside, New York 11104

February 12

Dear Miguel,

How are you? I'm fine. Here's a letter in English. It's good practice for you and me!

I have classes in English at La Guardia Community College. I'm in a class with eight students. They're all from different countries: Japan, Brazil, Switzerland, Poland, and Italy. Our teacher's name is Isabel. She's very nice and a very good teacher.

I live in an apartment with two American girls, Annie and Marnie Kass. They are sisters. Annie's twenty years old and a dancer. Marnie's eighteen and a student. They're very friendly, but it isn't easy to understand them. They speak very fast!

New York is very big, very exciting but very expensive! The subway isn't difficult to use and it's cheap. It's very cold now but Central Park is lovely in the snow. I'm very happy here.

Write to me soon.
Love,
Dorita

EVERYDAY ENGLISH

In a café

1 1 **T 2.7** Read and listen to the prices.

£1.00 one pound	50p fifty p /piː/	£10.75 ten pounds seventy-five
£5.00 five pounds	£7.50 seven pounds fifty	

2 **T 2.8** Write the prices you hear. Practise saying them.

2 Read the menu. Match the food and pictures.

Baker Street Snack Bar

Menu

Hamburger & chips	£3.50
Chicken & chips	£3.90
Tuna & egg salad	£4.25
Pizza	£3.75
Ice-cream	£1.50
Chocolate cake	£1.75
Coffee	£1.00
Tea	60p
Orange juice	90p
Mineral water	70p

3 [T 2.9] Listen and repeat. Then ask and answer questions with a partner.

> *How much is a hamburger and chips?*

> *Three pounds fifty.*

> *How much is a hamburger and chips and an orange juice?*

> *Four pounds forty.*

4 [T 2.10] Listen and complete the conversations.

A Good morning.
B Good _____ . Can I have _____ , please?
A Here you are. Anything else?
B No, thanks.
A _____ p, please.
B Thanks.
A Thank you.

A Hi. Can I help?
B Yes. Can I have a _____ salad, please?
A Anything to drink?
B Yeah. A _____ , please.
A OK. Here you are.
B _____ is that?
A _____ pounds _____ , please.
B Thanks.

5 Practise the conversations with your partner.
Make more conversations.

3 The world of work

Present Simple 1 – *he/she/it* · Questions and negatives · Jobs · What time is it?

STARTER

What are the jobs of the people in your family? Tell the class.

My father is a doctor.

My mother is a …

My brother …

THREE JOBS
Present Simple *he/she/it*

1 **T 3.1** Listen and read about Ali and Bob.

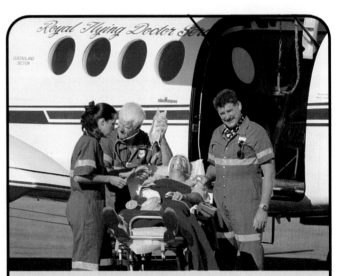

Bob is a doctor. He's English but now he lives in Australia in the small town of Alice Springs. He isn't an ordinary doctor, he's a *flying* doctor. Every day, from 8 a.m. to 10 a.m. he speaks to people on his radio, then he flies to help them. He works 16 hours a day non-stop but he loves his job. He isn't married. He has no free time.

Bob Nelson

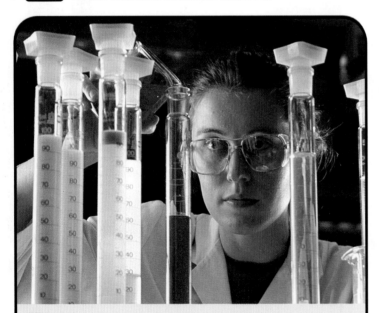

Ali is a scientist. She comes from Cambridge in England but now she lives in Switzerland. She works three days a week at the Institute of Molecular Biology in Geneva. She speaks three languages: English, French, and German. She's married and has a daughter. She likes skiing in winter and going for walks in summer.

Alison Hauser

GRAMMAR SPOT
1 <u>Underline</u> all the verbs in the texts. *is   comes*
2 What is the last letter of these verbs?
3 Practise saying the verbs. Read the texts aloud.

2 Complete the sentences about Ali and Bob.

1 She's a scientist. He <u>'s a</u> doctor.
2 Alison comes from England. Bob _____ _____ England, too.
3 She lives in a big city, but he _____ in a _____ town.
4 She _____ three days _____ week. He _____ 16 hours a day _____ .
5 He _____ to sick people on his radio. She _____ three languages.
6 She loves her job and he _____ _____ _____ , too.
7 She _____ _____ daughter. He _____ married.
8 She _____ skiing and going _____ walks in her free time. He never _____ free time.

T 3.2 Listen and check.

PRACTICE

Talking about people

1 Read the information about Philippe.

Philippe Ballon	
Job	a barman
Country	France
Town	Paris
Place of work	in the centre of Paris
Languages	French, a little English
Married?	no
Family	a dog (!)
Free time	walking his dog, playing football

2 Talk about Phillippe.

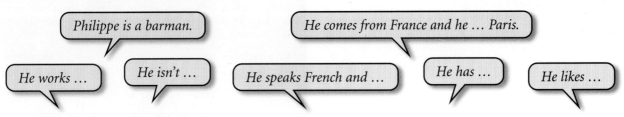

Philippe is a barman.

He comes from France and he ... Paris.

He works ...

He isn't ...

He speaks French and ...

He has ...

He likes ...

3 Write about a friend or a relative. Talk to a partner about him/her.
My friend Anna is a student. She lives in ...

WHAT DOES SHE DO?
Questions and negatives

1 [**T 3.3**] Read and listen. Complete the answers. Practise the questions and answers.

Where does Alison come from?	Cambridge, _____ England.
What does she do?	She's _____ scientist.
Does she speak French?	_____ , she does.
Does she speak Spanish?	_____ , she doesn't.

GRAMMAR SPOT

1 What does she/he do? = What's her/his job?

2 Complete these sentences with the correct form of *come*.

Positive
She _____ from England.
Negative
She _____ _____ from America.
Question
Where _____ she _____ from?

3 Notice the pronunciation of *does* and *doesn't*.
/dəz/   /dʌz/   /'dʌznt/
Does he speak French? Yes he **does**./No, he **doesn't**.

▶▶ **Grammar Reference 3.1 p.126**

---

2 Complete the questions and answers.

1 Where _____ Bob _____ from?
England.
2 What _____ he _____ ?
He's a doctor.
3 _____ he fly to help people?
Yes, he _____ .
4 _____ he _____ French and German?
No, he _____ .

[**T 3.4**] Listen and check.

3 Write similar questions about Philippe the barman. Ask and answer with a partner.

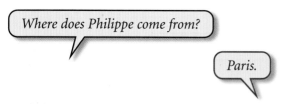

Where does Philippe come from?

Paris.

PRACTICE

Asking about people

1 Read the information about Keiko or Mark.

Keiko Wilson

Job	an interpreter
Country	Japan
Town	New York
Place of work	at the United Nations
Languages	Japanese, English, and French
Family	married to an American, two sons
Free time	skiing

2 Talk to a partner.

Keiko's an interpreter. She comes from Japan. She lives ...

3 Write questions about Keiko or Mark.

- Where/come from?
  Where does Keiko come from?
- Where/live?
- What/do?
- Where/work?
- Does he/she speak French/Spanish . . . ?
- What . . . in his/her free time?
- . . . listen to music?
- How many children . . . ?
- . . . a dog?

4 Don't look at the information. Ask and answer questions with your partner.

5 Now ask your partner the same questions about a friend or relative.

Listening and pronunciation

6 **T 3.5** Listen to the sentences about Philippe, Keiko, and Mark. Correct the wrong sentences.

> *Philippe comes from Paris.*

> *Yes, that's right.*

> *Philippe lives in London.*

> *No, he doesn't. He lives in Paris.*

7 **T 3.6** Tick (✓) the sentence you hear.

1. ☐ He likes his job.
   ☐ She likes her job.
2. ☐ She loves walking.
   ☐ She loves working.
3. ☐ He's married.
   ☐ He isn't married.
4. ☐ Does she have three children?
   ☐ Does he have three children?
5. ☐ What does he do?
   ☐ Where does he go?

Check it

8 Tick (✓) the correct sentence.

1. ☐ She comes from Japan.
   ☐ She come from Japan.
2. ☐ What he do in his free time?
   ☐ What does he do in his free time?
3. ☐ Where lives she?
   ☐ Where does she live?
4. ☐ He isn't married.
   ☐ He doesn't married.
5. ☐ Does she has two sons?
   ☐ Does she have two sons?
6. ☐ He doesn't play football.
   ☐ He no plays football.
7. ☐ She doesn't love Peter.
   ☐ She doesn't loves Peter.
8. ☐ What's he's address?
   ☐ What's his address?

Mark König

Job	a journalist for the BBC
Country	England
Town	Moscow
Place of work	in an office
Languages	English, Russian, and German
Family	married, three daughters
Free time	listening to music

1 **Seumas McSporran** /'ʃeɪməs mək'spɒrən/ comes from Scotland. Look at the photographs of some of the things he does every day.

6.00 a.m.

8.00 a.m.

The man with thirteen jobs

9.00 a.m.

10.00 a.m.

12.00 a.m.

2.00 p.m.

3.00 p.m.

5.00 p.m.

2 Match a sentence with a photograph.
1 He **helps** in the shop.
2 He **makes** breakfast for the hotel guests.
3 He **serves** petrol.
4 He **delivers** the beer to the pub.
5 He **collects** the post from the boat.
6 He **drives** the children to school.
7 He **delivers** the letters.
8 He **has** a glass of wine.
9 He **works** as an undertaker.

Seumas McSporran

is a very busy man. He is 60 years old and he has thirteen jobs. He is a postman, a policeman, a fireman, a taxi driver, a school-bus driver, a boatman, an ambulance man, an accountant, a petrol attendant, a barman, and an undertaker. Also, he and his wife, Margaret, have a shop and a small hotel.

Seumas lives and works on the island of Gigha in the west of Scotland. Only 120 people live on Gigha but in summer 150 tourists come by boat every day.

Every weekday Seumas gets up at 6.00 and makes breakfast for the hotel guests. At 8.00 he drives the island's children to school. At 9.00 he collects the post from the boat and delivers it to all the houses on the island. He also delivers the beer to the island's only pub. Then he helps Margaret in the shop.

He says: 'Margaret likes being busy, too. We never have holidays and we don't like watching television. In the evenings Margaret makes supper and I do the accounts. At 10.00 we have a glass of wine and then we go to bed. Perhaps our life isn't very exciting, but we like it.'

10.00 p.m.

3 Read about Seumas. Answer the questions.
1 Where does Seumas live?
2 How old is he?
3 How many jobs does he have?
4 What's his wife's name?
5 What does she do?
6 How many people live on Gigha?
7 How many tourists visit Gigha in summer?
8 What does Seumas do in the morning?
9 What do he and Margaret do in the evening?

4 Look at the photos. Ask and answer questions with a partner about times in Seumas's day.

> *What does he do at 6 o'clock?*

> *He gets up and makes breakfast.*

5 **T 3.7** Listen to four conversations from Seumas's day. After each one answer these questions.
1 Is it morning, afternoon, or evening?
2 Who are the people? Where are they?
3 What is Seumas's job?

6 Complete the conversations.

1 A Good _____ . Can I _____ two ice-creams, please?
   B Chocolate or vanilla?
   A One chocolate, one vanilla please.
   B That's _____ . Anything _____ ?
   A No, thank you.

2 A Only _____ letters for you this _____ , Mrs Craig.
   B Thank you very much, Mr McSporran. And _____ 's Mrs McSporran this _____ ?
   A Oh, she's very well, thank you. She's _____ in the shop.

3 A A glass of _____ before bed, my dear?
   B Oh, yes please.
   A _____ you are.
   B Thank you, my dear. I'm very _____ this _____ .

4 A Hello, Mr McSporran!
   B Good _____ , boys and girls. Hurry up, we're late.
   A Can I sit here, Mr McSporran?
   C No, no, I _____ to sit there.
   B Be quiet _____ of you, and SIT DOWN!

Practise the conversations with your partner.

VOCABULARY AND PRONUNCIATION
Jobs

1 Use your dictionary and match a picture with a job in column **A**.

1 **d**

2

3

4

5

6

7

8

9

A	B
a A pilot	designs buildings.
b An interpreter	delivers letters.
c A nurse	looks after people in hospital.
d A barman	looks after money.
e An accountant	writes for a newspaper.
f A journalist	translates things.
g A postman	sells things.
h An architect	flies planes.
i A shopkeeper	serves drinks.

2 Match a job in **A** with a line in **B**.

3 Look at the phonetic spelling of some of the words. Practise saying them.

1 /nɜːs/   2 /ˈpəʊsmən/   3 /əˈkaʊntənt/   4 /ˈʃɒpkiːpə/   5 /ˈɑːkɪtekt/   6 /ˈbɑːmən/

4 Memorize the jobs. Close your books. Ask and answer questions with a partner.

What does a pilot do?

He/She flies planes.

EVERYDAY ENGLISH
What time is it?

1 Look at the clocks. Write the times. Practise saying them.

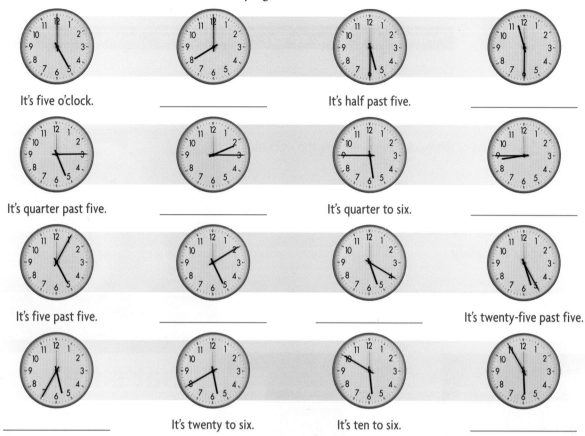

It's five o'clock.   _____   It's half past five.   _____

It's quarter past five.   _____   It's quarter to six.   _____

It's five past five.   _____   _____   It's twenty-five past five.

_____   It's twenty to six.   It's ten to six.   _____

T 3.8 Listen and check.

2 Look at the times.

It's about three o'clock.   It's about five o'clock.

What time is it now? What time does the lesson end?

3 **T 3.9** Listen and practise the conversations.

Conversation 1

Excuse me. Can you tell me the time, please?

Yes, of course. It's (about) six o'clock.

Thanks.

Conversation 2

Excuse me. Can you tell me the time, please?

I'm sorry, I don't know. I don't have a watch.

Never mind.

With a partner, draw clocks on a piece of paper. Make more conversations.

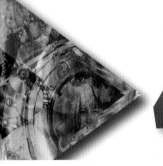

4 Take it easy!

Present Simple 2 – *I/you/we/they* · Leisure activities · Social expressions

STARTER

1 What year is it? What month is it? What day is it today?

2 Say the days of the week. Which days are the weekend?

WEEKDAYS AND WEEKENDS
Present Simple *I/you/we/they*

1 Read about Bobbi Brown's weekends. Complete the text with the verbs.

gets up lives is loves works doesn't work interviews starts

'What's free time?'
says Bobbi Brown.

Bobbi's weekends

Bobbi Brown _____ in New Jersey. She _____ thirty-four and _____ for SKY TV in New York City. But she _____ on weekdays, she only works at weekends. She _____ famous people for an early morning news programme called *The World This Weekend*. On Saturdays and Sundays she _____ at 3.00 in the morning because she _____ work at 6.30! She _____ her job because it is exciting.

2 **T 4.1** Now read and listen to what Bobbi says about her weekdays.

" *My weekends are fast and exciting. My weekdays are fast and domestic! I _____ two sons, Dylan, 7, and Dakota, 5. Every morning I _____ one hour before them, at 6.00, and I _____ to the gym. I _____ home and I _____ breakfast, then I _____ them to school. On Mondays I always _____ . I _____ all the food for the week. I often _____ dinner in the evenings, but not every day because I don't _____ cooking. Fortunately, my husband, Don, _____ cooking. On Tuesdays and Thursdays I _____ my father. He _____ on the next block. Every afternoon I _____ the kids from school. In the evenings Don and I usually _____ , but sometimes we _____ friends. We never _____ on Friday evenings because I _____ work so early on Saturdays.* "

3 Complete the text with the correct form of the verbs in the box. Look up new words in your dictionary.

> love   relax   have   like   go   live   start   come
> visit x2   go shopping   pick up   go out   get up   take
> buy   make   cook

T 4.1 Listen again and check. Read the text aloud.

Questions and negatives

4 **T 4.2** Read and listen. Complete Bobbi's answers. Practise the questions and answers.

Where do you work?	_____ New York.
Do you like your work?	Yes, I _____ .
Do you relax at weekends?	No, I _____ .
Why don't you relax at weekends?	_____ I work.

5 Work in pairs. One of you is Bobbi Brown. Ask and answer questions about your life.

- Where . . . you live/work?
- Are . . . married?
- Do . . . have children?
- What time . . . get up/Saturday morning/Monday morning?
- Why . . . get up at . . . ? Because I . . .
- . . . like your work?
- Why . . . like it? Because it . . .
- . . . like cooking?
- . . . your husband like cooking?
- Who . . . you visit on Tuesdays and Thursdays?
- Where . . . your father live?
- . . . go out on Friday evenings? Why not?
- . . . have a busy life?

GRAMMAR SPOT

1 Complete the table for the Present Simple.

	Positive	Negative
I	work	don't work
You	_____	_____
He/She	_____	_____
It	_____	_____
We	_____	_____
They	_____	_____

2 Complete the questions and answers.

Where _____ you work?
Where _____ she work?
_____ you work in New York? Yes, I _____ .
_____ he work in New York? No, he _____ .

3 Find the words in the text:
always usually often sometimes never

▶▶ **Grammar Reference 4.1 and 4.2 p127**

PRACTICE

Talking about you

1 Make the questions. Then match the questions and answers.

Questions		Answers
1 What time	do you like your job?	a My mother and sisters.
2 Where	do you travel to school?	b To Spain or Portugal.
3 What	do you go on holiday?	c After dinner.
4 When	do you go to bed?	d At 11 o'clock.
5 Who	you go out on Friday evenings?	e I always relax.
6 Why	do you live with?	f Because it's interesting.
7 How	do you do on Sundays?	g By bus.
8 Do	do you do your homework?	h Yes, I do sometimes.

T 4.3 Listen and check.

2 Ask and answer the questions with a partner. Give true answers.

3 Tell the class about you and your partner.

> *Maria gets up at half past eight. I get up at 8.00 on weekdays but at 11.00 at weekends.*

> *I live with my parents and my grandmother. Maria lives with her parents, too.*

Listening and pronunciation

4 **T 4.4** Tick (✓) the sentence you hear.

1 ☐ What does he do on Sundays?
  ☐ What does she do on Sundays?

2 ☐ Do you stay home on Tuesday evenings?
  ☐ Do you stay home on Thursday evenings?

3 ☐ He lives here.
  ☐ He leaves here.

4 ☐ Where do you go on Saturday evenings?
  ☐ What do you do on Saturday evenings?

5 ☐ I read a lot.
  ☐ I eat a lot.

6 ☐ Why do you like your job?
  ☐ Why don't you like your job?

A questionnaire

5 Read the questionnaire on p31. Answer the questions about you. Put ✓ or ✗ in column 1.

6 Ask your teacher the questions, then ask two students. Complete columns 2, 3, and 4.

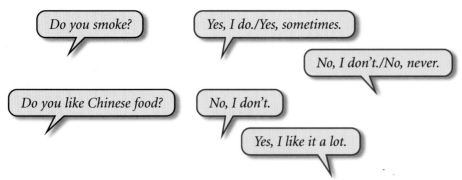

> *Do you smoke?*

> *Yes, I do./Yes, sometimes.*

> *No, I don't./No, never.*

> *Do you like Chinese food?*

> *No, I don't.*

> *Yes, I like it a lot.*

7 Use the information in the questionnaire. Write about you and your teacher.
I don't get up early on weekdays, but my teacher does. We don't play tennis ...

A Questionnaire

HOW DO YOU LIVE?

Do you ... ?

	Me	T	S1	S2
get up early on weekdays	☐	☐	☐	☐
play tennis	☐	☐	☐	☐
smoke	☐	☐	☐	☐
drink wine	☐	☐	☐	☐
like Chinese food	☐	☐	☐	☐
watch TV a lot	☐	☐	☐	☐
have a big breakfast	☐	☐	☐	☐
have a computer	☐	☐	☐	☐

Positives and negatives

8 Make the sentences opposite.

1 She's French. **She isn't French.**
2 I don't like cooking. **I like cooking.**
3 She doesn't speak Spanish.
4 They want to learn English.
5 We're tired and want to go to bed.
6 Roberto likes watching football on TV, but he doesn't like playing it.
7 I work at home because I have a computer.
8 Amelia isn't happy because she doesn't have a new car.
9 I smoke, I drink, and I don't go to bed early.
10 He doesn't smoke, he doesn't drink, and he goes to bed early.

READING AND LISTENING
My favourite season

1 1 What season is it now? What are the seasons?
   2 What month is it now? Say the months of the year.
   3 When are the different seasons in your country?

2 Look at the photographs. Which season is it? What colours do you see?

3 **T 4.5** Read and listen to three people from different countries.

AL WHEELER
from Canada

We have long, cold winters and short, hot summers. We have a holiday home near a lake, so in summer I go sailing a lot and I play baseball, but in winter I often play ice hockey and go ice-skating. My favourite season is autumn, or fall, as we say in North America. I love the colours of the trees – red, gold, orange, yellow, and brown.

MANUELA DA SILVA
from Portugal

People think it's always warm and sunny in Portugal, but January and February are often cold, wet, and grey. I don't like winter. I usually meet friends in restaurants and bars and we chat. Sometimes we go to a Brazilian bar. I love Brazilian music. But then suddenly it's summer and at weekends we drive to the beach, sunbathe, and go swimming. I love summer.

TOSHI SUZUKI from Japan

I work for Pentax cameras, in the export department. I don't have a lot of free time, but I have one special hobby – taking photographs, of course! I like taking photographs of flowers, especially in spring. Sometimes, after work, I relax in a bar near my office with friends. My friend, Shigeru, likes singing pop songs in the bar. This has a special name, 'karaoke'. I don't sing – I'm too shy!

4 Answer the questions.

1 Do they all play sports?
2 What do Al and Manuela do in winter?
3 Do Manuela and Toshi like going to bars?
4 Where is Al's holiday home?
5 When does Toshi like taking photographs of flowers?

6 What do Manuela and her friends do in summer?
7 Do you know all their jobs?
8 Why does Al like autumn?
9 Why doesn't Toshi sing in the bar?
10 Which colours are in the texts?

5 There are six mistakes about Al, Manuela, and Toshi. Correct them.

Al comes from Canada. In winter he plays ice hockey and goes skiing. He has a holiday home near the sea.	**Manuela** comes from Brazil. She likes sunbathing and sailing in summer.	**Toshi** comes from Japan. He has a lot of free time. He likes taking photographs and singing pop songs in bars.

6 **T 4.6** Listen to the conversations. Is it Al, Manuela, or Toshi? Where are they? How do you know? Discuss with a partner.

What do you think?

- What is *your* favourite season? Why?
- What do you do in the different seasons?

VOCABULARY AND SPEAKING
Leisure activities

1 Match the words and pictures. Tick (✓) the things that *you* like doing.

- [ ] playing football
- [ ] dancing
- [ ] skiing
- [ ] watching TV
- [ ] going to the gym
- [ ] taking photographs
- [ ] cooking
- [ ] playing computer games
- [ ] sailing
- [ ] listening to music
- [ ] swimming
- [ ] reading
- [ ] eating in restaurants
- [ ] going to the cinema
- [ ] jogging
- [ ] sunbathing

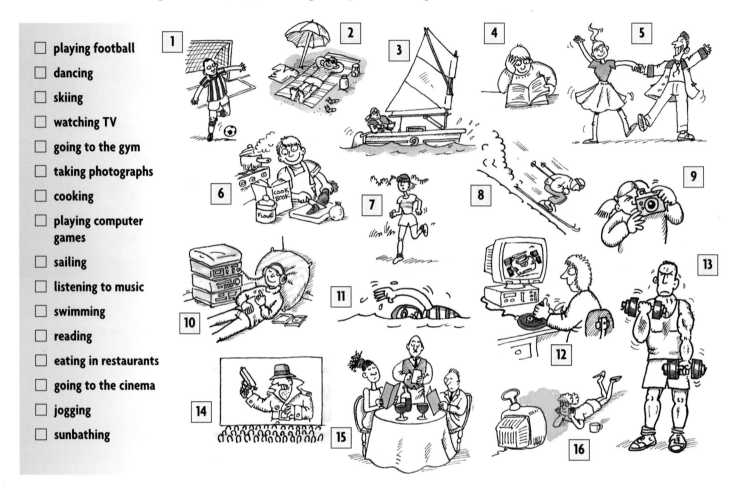

2 Discuss in groups what you think your teacher likes doing. Choose *five* activities.

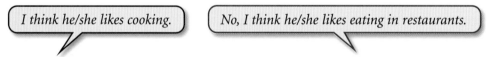

> *I think he/she likes cooking.*

> *No, I think he/she likes eating in restaurants.*

Ask your teacher questions to find out who is correct.

> *Do you like cooking?*

> *Do you like eating in restaurants?*

3 Tell the other students what you *like* doing and what you *don't like* doing from the list. Ask questions about the activities.

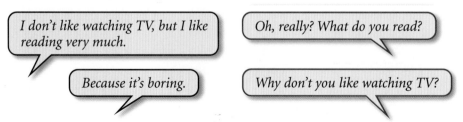

> *I don't like watching TV, but I like reading very much.*

> *Oh, really? What do you read?*

> *Because it's boring.*

> *Why don't you like watching TV?*

4 Tell the other students things you like doing which are *not* on the list.

EVERYDAY ENGLISH

Social expressions

1 Complete the conversations with the expressions.

1 **A** _____ . The traffic is bad today. **B** _____ . Come and sit down. We're on page 25.	Don't worry. I'm sorry I'm late.
2 **A** _____ . **B** Yes? **A** Do you have a dictionary? **B** _____ I don't. It's at home. **A** _____ .	I'm sorry, Excuse me. That's OK.
3 **A** It's very hot in here. _____ ? **B** _____ ? I'm quite cold. **A** OK. _____ .	Really? Can I open the window? It doesn't matter.
4 **A** _____ ! **B** Can I help you? **A** Can I have a film for my camera? **B** How many exposures? **A** _____ ? **B** How many *exposures*? **A** _____ ? **B** How many pictures? 24? 36? 40? **A** Ah! _____ ! 40, please.	Pardon? Now I understand! Excuse me! What does 'exposures' mean?

T 4.7 Listen and check.

2 Practise the conversations with a partner.

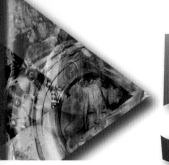

5 Where do you live?

There is/are · Prepositions · *some/any* · *this/that* · Furniture · Directions 1

STARTER

1 Write the words in the correct column.

an armchair   a fridge   a television
a coffee table   a shelf   a plant   a stereo
a lamp   a cooker   a washing machine
a telephone   a cupboard   a cup   a sofa

The living room	The kitchen	both

2 What's in your living room?
Tell a partner.

WHAT'S IN THE LIVING ROOM?
There is/are, prepositions

1 Helen has a new flat. Describe her living room on p37.

> *There's a telephone.*

> *There are two plants.*

2 **T 5.1** Read and listen. Complete the answers.
Practise the questions and answers.

Is there a television?	Yes, there _____ .
Is there a radio?	No, there _____ .
Are there any books?	Yes, there _____ .
How many books are there?	There _____ a lot.
Are there any photographs?	No, there _____ .

GRAMMAR SPOT

Complete the tables.

Positive

There	_____	a television.
	_____	some books.

Negative

There	_____	a radio.
	_____	any photos.

Question

_____	there	a television?
_____		any books?

▶▶ **Grammar Reference 5.1 and 5.2 p127**

3 Ask and answer questions about these things.

a dog	a cat	a computer
a fire	a mirror	a clock
a rug		

plants	pictures	bookshelves
lamps	newspapers	photos
flowers		

> *Is there a cat?*

> *Yes, there is.*

4 Look at the picture of Helen's living room.
Complete the sentences with a preposition.

on	under	next to	in front of

1 The television is _____ the cupboard.
2 The coffee table is _____ the sofa.
3 There are some magazines _____ the table.
4 The television is _____ the stereo.
5 There are two pictures _____ the walls.
6 The cat is _____ the rug _____ the fire.

Helen's living room

PRACTICE

What's in your picture?

1 Work with a partner. Look at the pictures from your teacher. There's a picture of another living room and lots of things that go in it. *Don't* look at your partner's picture.

Student A Your picture is not complete. Ask Student B questions and find out where the things go. Draw them on your picture.

Where's the lamp? Where exactly?

Student B Your picture is complete. Answer Student A's questions and help him/her complete the picture.

It's on the table. Next to the book.

2 **T 5.2** Look at the complete picture together. Listen to someone describing it. There are *five* mistakes in the description. Say 'Stop!' when you hear a mistake.

Stop! There aren't three people! There are four people!

WHAT'S IN THE KITCHEN?
some/any, this/that/these/those

1 This is the kitchen in Helen's new flat. Describe it.

Helen's kitchen

2 **T 5.3** Listen and complete the conversation between Helen and her friend, Bob.

Helen And this is the kitchen.

Bob Mmm, it's very nice.

Helen Well, it's not very big, but there _____ a _____ of cupboards. And _____ 's a new fridge, and a cooker. That's new, too.

Bob But what's *in* all these cupboards?

Helen Well, not a lot. There are some cups, but there aren't any plates. And I have _____ knives and forks, but I don't have _____ spoons!

Bob Do you have _____ glasses?

Helen No. Sorry.

Bob Never mind. We can drink this champagne from those cups! Cheers!

3 What is there in your kitchen? How is your kitchen different from Helen's?

1 What's the difference between the sentences?
   There are **two** magazines.
   There are **some** magazines.

2 When do we say *some*? When do we say *any*?
   There are **some** cups.
   There aren't **any** glasses.
   Are there **any** spoons?

3 Complete the sentences with *this, that, these,* or *those*.

1 I like _____ champagne. 3 _____ cooker is new.

2 _____ flowers are lovely. 4 Give me _____ cups.

▶▶ **Grammar Reference 5.3 and 5.4 p127**

PRACTICE

In our classroom

1 Complete the sentences with *some* or *any*.

1 In our classroom there are _____ books on the floor.
2 There aren't _____ plants.
3 Are there _____ Spanish students in your class?
4 There aren't _____ Chinese students.
5 We have _____ dictionaries in the cupboard.
6 There aren't _____ pens in my bag.

2 What is there in your classroom? Describe it.

3 Talk about things in your classroom, using *this/that/these/those*. Point to or hold the things.

This is my favourite pen.   *I like that bag.*

These chairs are nice.   *Those windows are dirty.*

What's in Pierre's briefcase?

4 **T 5.4** Pierre is a Frenchman on business in Boston. Listen to him describe what's in his briefcase. Tick (✓) the things in it.

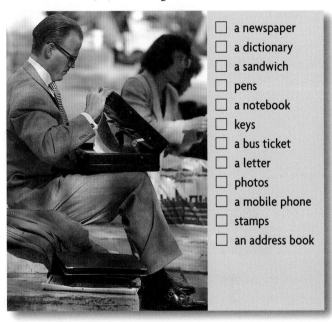

- [ ] a newspaper
- [ ] a dictionary
- [ ] a sandwich
- [ ] pens
- [ ] a notebook
- [ ] keys
- [ ] a bus ticket
- [ ] a letter
- [ ] photos
- [ ] a mobile phone
- [ ] stamps
- [ ] an address book

5 Look in your bag. Ask and answer questions about your bags with a partner.

Is there a dictionary in your bag?

Are there any stamps?   *How many stamps are there?*

Check it

6 Tick (✓) the correct sentence.

1 ☐ There aren't some sandwiches.
  ☐ There aren't any sandwiches.
2 ☐ Do you have some good dictionary?
  ☐ Do you have a good dictionary?
3 ☐ I have some photos of my dog.
  ☐ I have any photos of my dog.
4 ☐ I have lot of books.
  ☐ I have a lot of books.
5 ☐ How many students are there in this class?
  ☐ How many of students are there in this class?
6 ☐ Next my house there's a park.
  ☐ Next to my house there's a park.
7 ☐ Look at this house over there!
  ☐ Look at that house over there!
  ☐ Henry, that is my mother. Mum, that is Henry.
  ☐ Henry, this is my mother. Mum, this is Henry.

READING AND SPEAKING
At home on a plane

1 Write the words in the correct place on the picture. What other things are there on a plane?

steps   a cockpit   a flight attendant   the first class section   emergency exit   windows   door   toilet

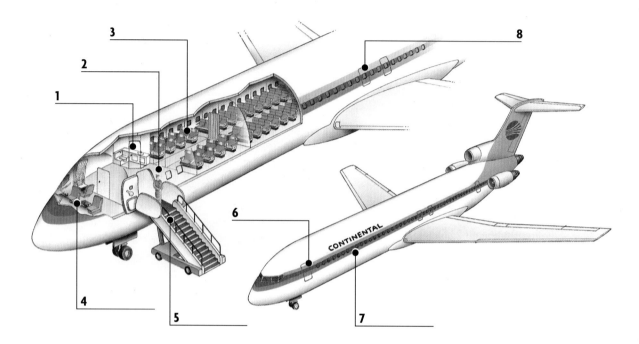

2 Read about Joanne Ussery and answer the questions.
1 How old is she?
2 Where does she live?
3 How old is her home?
4 How many grandsons does she have?
5 How many bedrooms are there?
6 How many toilets are there?

3 Are the sentences true (✓) or false (✗)?
1 Joanne loves her home.
2 You need a ticket when you visit her.
3 The bathroom is next to the living room.
4 Joanne sometimes opens the emergency exit doors.
5 There is a photo of the plane in the living room.
6 It's very warm in summer because she doesn't have air conditioning.
7 Her friends love her parties because flight attendants serve the drinks.
8 She doesn't want to buy another plane.

4 Work with a partner. Ask and answer questions about Joanne's home.

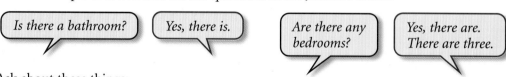

Is there a bathroom?   Yes, there is.   Are there any bedrooms?   Yes, there are. There are three.

Ask about these things:
• a telephone   • a dishwasher   • toilets   • flight attendants   • an upstairs bedroom

What do you think?

What do you like about Joanne's home? What don't you like?

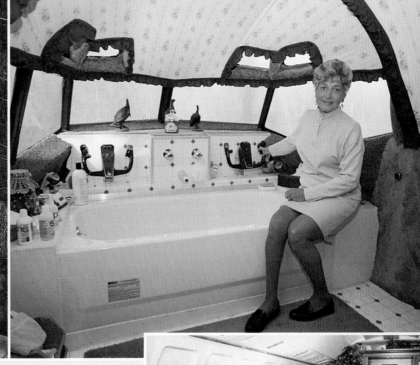

The lady who lives on a plane

Joanne Ussery, 54, from Mississippi is a big favourite with her two grandsons because she lives on a jet plane. Her home is a Boeing 727, so a visit to grandma is very special.

Joanne's front door is at the top of the plane's steps, but you don't need a ticket or a passport when you visit. There are three bedrooms, a living room, a modern kitchen, and a luxury bathroom. The bathroom is in the cockpit, with the bath under the windows. Next to this is Joanne's bedroom in the first class section of the plane. Then there's the living room with four emergency exit doors, which she opens on summer evenings. On the wall there's a photo of the plane flying for Continental Airlines from Florida to the Caribbean. There are also four toilets, all with No Smoking signs.

'The plane is 27 years old and it's the best home in the world,' says Joanne. 'It has all the things you want in a home: a telephone, air conditioning, a cooker, a washing machine, even a dishwasher. It's always very warm, even in winter, and it's very big, 42 metres long. My grandchildren love running up and down. And my friends love parties here, but there aren't any flight attendants to serve them their drinks!'

The plane cost Joanne just $2,000. 'Next time,' she says, 'I want a Boeing 747, not a 727, because they have an upstairs and a downstairs, and I want to go upstairs to bed!' ✈

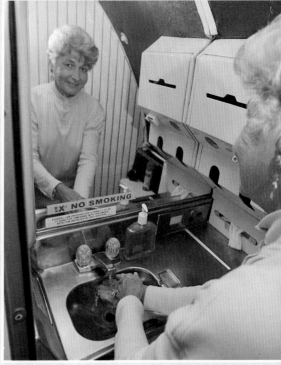

LISTENING AND SPEAKING
Homes around the world

1 Match the places and the photos. What do you know about them?

☐ Lisbon ☐ Toronto ☐ Malibu ☐ Samoa

2 **T 5.5** Listen to some people from these places. Complete the chart.

c

d

a

b

	Manola from LISBON	**Ray and Elsie** from TORONTO	**Brad** from MALIBU	**Alise** from SAMOA
House or flat?				
Old or modern?				
Where?				
How many bedrooms?				
Live(s) with?				
Extra information				

3 Talk about where you live.

Do you live in a house or a flat?

Where is it?

How many rooms are there?

Do you have a garden?

Who do you live with?

4 Write a paragraph about where you live.

EVERYDAY ENGLISH
Directions 1

1 Look at the street map. Where can you buy these things?

> some aspirin   a CD   a plane ticket   a newspaper   a book   some stamps

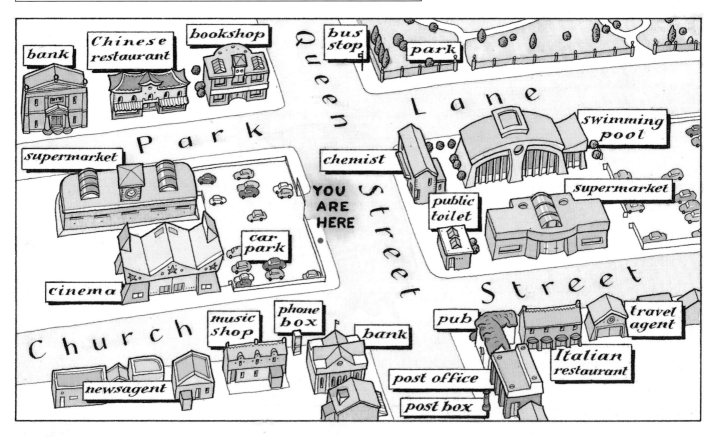

2 **T 5.6** Listen to the conversations and complete them.

1 **A** Excuse me! Is _____ a chemist _____ here?
  B Yes. It's over _____ .
  A Thanks.

2 **A** _____ me! Is there a _____ near here?
  B Yes. _____ _____ Church Street. Take the first _____ _____
    _____ right. It's _____ _____ the music shop.
  A Oh yes. Thanks.

3 **A** Excuse me! Is there a _____ near here?
  B There's a Chinese one in Park Lane _____ _____ the bank, and
    there's an Italian one in Church Street next to the _____ _____ .
  A Is that one _____ ?
  B No. Just two minutes, that's all.

4 **A** Is there a post office near here?
  B Go straight ahead, and it's _____ _____ left, _____ _____ the pub.
  A Thanks a lot.

Practise the conversations with a partner.

3 Make more conversations with your partner. Ask and answer about these places:

- a bookshop
- a cinema
- a bank
- a phone box
- a public toilet
- a music shop
- a supermarket
- a bus stop
- a park
- a swimming pool
- a post box
- a pub

4 Talk about where *you* are. Is there a chemist near here? Is it far? What about a bank/a post office/ a supermarket?

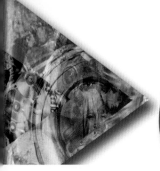

6 Can you speak English?

can/can't/could/couldn't · was/were · Words that sound the same · On the phone

STARTER

1 Where do people speak these languages?

French Spanish German Italian Portuguese Japanese English

> *They speak French in France and also in Canada.*

2 Which languages can you speak?
Tell the class.

> *I can speak English and a little Spanish. And of course, I can speak my language.*

WHAT CAN YOU DO?
can/can't

1 **T 6.1** Match the sentences and pictures. Then listen and check.

1 He can ski really well.
2 She can use a computer.
3 'Can dogs swim?' 'Yes, they can.'
4 'Can you speak Japanese?' 'No, I can't.'
5 I can't spell your name.
6 We can't understand the question.

a	

b	

c	

d	

e	

f	

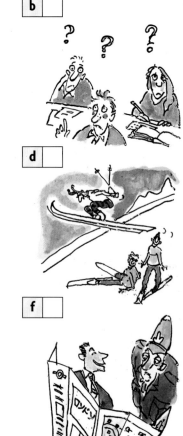

GRAMMAR SPOT

1 Say all persons of *can* and *can't*.
I can, you can, he ... she ... it ... we ...
they ...
I can't, you ..., etc.
What do you notice?

2 **T 6.2** Listen and repeat these sentences.

I can speak French.
Can you speak French?   = /kən/
Yes, I can.   = /kæn/
No, I can't.   = /kɑːnt/

3 Say these sentences.

● ● ●   ● ● ●
We can swim.   She can't cook.

▶▶ **Grammar Reference 6.1 p128**

2 **T 6.3** Listen and complete the sentences with *can* or *can't* + verb.

1 I _____ _____ _____ , but I _____ _____ _____ .
2 He _____ _____ , but he _____ _____ .
3 '_____ you _____ ?' 'Yes, I _____ .'
4 They _____ _____ , but they _____ _____ .
5 We _____ _____ and we _____ _____ .
6 '_____ she _____ ?' 'No, she _____ .'

PRACTICE

Tina can't cook. Can you?

1 **T 6.4** Listen to Tina and complete the chart. Put ✓ or ✗.

Can ...?	Tina	you	your partner
drive a car			
speak French			
speak Italian			
cook			
play tennis			
ski			
swim			
play the piano			
use a computer			

2 Complete the chart about you.

3 Complete the chart about your partner. Ask and answer the questions.

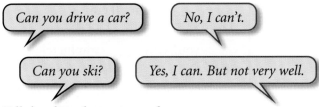

Can you drive a car?   No, I can't.

Can you ski?   Yes, I can. But not very well.

Tell the class about you and your partner.

Louis can ski, but I can't.

What can computers do?

4 Talk about computers with a partner. What can they do? What can't they do?

They can translate, but they can't speak English.

Yes, they can.

COMPUTERS

Can they . . . ?

- translate
- write poetry
- speak English
- laugh
- play chess
- hear
- check spellings
- feel
- make music
- think
- have conversations
- fall in love

5 What can people do that computers can't do?

WHERE WERE YOU YESTERDAY?
was/were, can/could

Read the questions. Complete the answers.

Present	Past
1 What day is it today? It's _____ .	What day was it yesterday? It was _____ .
2 What month is it now? It's _____ .	What month was it last month? It was _____ .
3 Where are you now? I'm in/at _____ .	Where were you yesterday? I was in/at _____ .
4 Are you in England? _____ , I am. _____ , I'm not.	Were you in England in 1999? _____ , I was. _____ , I wasn't.
5 Can you swim? _____ , I can. _____ , I can't.	Could you swim when you were five? _____ , I could. _____ , I couldn't.
6 Can your teacher speak three languages? Yes, _____ can. No, _____ can't.	Could your teacher speak English when he/she was seven? Yes, _____ could. No, _____ couldn't.

GRAMMAR SPOT

1 Complete the table with the past of *to be*.

	Positive	Negative
I	was	wasn't
You	were	weren't
He/She/It	_____	_____
We	_____	_____
They	_____	_____

2 **T 6.5** Listen and repeat.

/wəz/   /wə/

It was Monday yesterday. We were at school.

In short answers the pronunciation is different.

                        /wɒz/

'Was it hot?'   'Yes, it was.'

                        /wɜː/

'Were you tired?'   'Yes, we were.'

3 What is the past of *can*?

Positive _____   **Negative** _____

▶▶ **Grammar Reference 6.1 and 6.2 p128**

PRACTICE

Talking about you

1 Ask and answer questions with a partner.

Where were you . . . ?

- at eight o'clock this morning
- at half past six yesterday evening
- at two o'clock this morning
- at this time yesterday
- at ten o'clock last night
- last Saturday evening

2 Complete the conversation, using *was, were, wasn't, weren't,* or *couldn't.*

Kim	_____ you at Charlotte's party last Saturday?
Max	Yes, I _____ .
Kim	_____ it good?
Max	Well, it _____ OK.
Kim	_____ there many people?
Max	Yes, there _____ .
Kim	_____ Henry there?
Max	No, he _____ . And where _____ you? Why _____ you there?
Kim	Oh ... I _____ go because I _____ at Mark's party! It _____ brilliant!

T 6.6 Listen and check. Listen for the pronunciation of *was* and *were*. Practise with a partner.

Four geniuses!

3 The people in the photos were all geniuses. Who are they?

4 Look at these sentences.

I was born in London in 1973. I could read when I was four.
My sister couldn't read until she was seven.

Match lines in **A**, **B**, and **C** and make similar sentences about the four geniuses.

A	B	C
Mozart / born in	Siberia / 1938	paint / one
Picasso / born in	Germany / 1879	dance / two
Nureyev / born in	Austria / 1756	play the piano / three
Einstein / born in	Spain / 1881	couldn't speak / eight

5 Ask and answer questions with a partner about the geniuses.

> When was Mozart born?

> Where was he born?

> How old was he when he could … ?

6 Work in groups. Ask and answer questions about you.

1 Where were you born?
2 When were you born?
3 How old were you when you could … ?
   • walk   • talk
   • read   • swim
   • ride a bike   • use a computer
   • speak a foreign language

Check it

7 Tick (✓) the correct sentence.

1 ☐ I don't can use a computer.
  ☐ I can't use a computer.

2 ☐ Was they at the party?
  ☐ Were they at the party?

3 ☐ I'm sorry. I can't go to the party.
  ☐ I'm sorry. I no can go to the party.

4 ☐ She was no at home.
  ☐ She wasn't at home.

5 ☐ He could play chess when he was five.
  ☐ He can play chess when he was five.

6 ☐ I can to speak English very well.
  ☐ I can speak English very well.

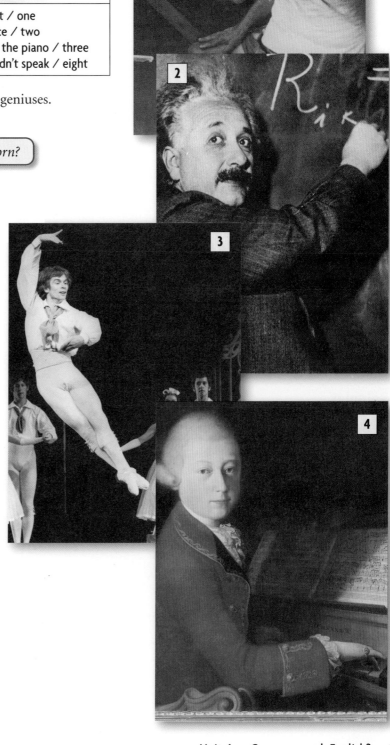

READING AND SPEAKING
Super Kids

1 Look at the children in the photographs. How old are they? What can they do?

2 Work in two groups.
   Group A Read about little Miss Picasso.
   Group B Read about the new Mozart.

3 Answer the questions about Alexandra or Lukas.
   1 How old is she/he?
   2 Why is she/he special?
   3 Where was she/he born?
   4 Where does she/he live now?
   5 Who does she/he live with?
   6 Does she/he go to school?
   7 What could she/he do when she/he was very young?
   8 Does she/he have much free time? Why not?
   9 Is she/he poor?
  10 Where was she/he last year?

4 Find a partner from the other group. Tell your partner about your child, using your answers.

5 What is the same about Alexandra and Lukas? What is different? Discuss with your partner.

They are both geniuses.

Alexandra is a painter, and Lukas is a pianist.

Roleplay

6 Work with a partner.
   Student A is a journalist.
   Student B is Alexandra or Lukas.

   Ask and answer questions, using the questions in exercise 3 to help you.

Hello, Alexandra! Can I ask you one or two questions?

Of course.

First of all, how old are you?

I'm thirteen.

The New **Mozart**

Ten-year-old **Lukas Vondracek** is very shy, but every year he travels the world and meets hundreds of people. Lukas is a brilliant pianist and he gives lots of concerts. Last year he was in Washington, Chicago, and London. He is sometimes called '**the new Mozart**'. He says 'I'm shy, but I love giving concerts.'

Lukas was born in **Opava** in the **Czech Republic** but now he lives with his parents in **Vienna**, where he practises the piano six hours a day. He goes to school two days a week. Lukas could play the piano when he was two and he could read music before he could read books. Now he can write music, too.

Lukas doesn't just play the piano, he plays football and ice hockey. He says: 'Mozart was poor and he couldn't play football, so I'm not like him at all!'

Little **Miss Picasso**

Alexandra Nechita is thirteen and she is called 'the new Picasso'. She paints large pictures in cubist style and sells them for between $10,000 and $80,000.

She was born in **Romania** but now she lives in **Los Angeles** with her family. She could paint very well when she was only four but her parents couldn't understand her pictures. Alexandra says: 'I paint how I feel, sometimes I'm happy and sometimes sad. I can't stop painting.' Every day after school she does her homework, plays with her little brother, then paints for two or three hours until bedtime.

Alexandra doesn't spend her money, she saves it: 'We were very poor when we were first in America. We couldn't buy many things, but now I can buy a big house for my family and we can travel the world. Last year we were in London, Paris, and Rome. It was fantastic!'

VOCABULARY AND PRONUNCIATION
Words that sound the same

1 Look at the sentences. What do you notice about these words?

I have a black **eye**.
No, he doesn't **know** the answer.

2 Find the words in **B** that have the same pronunciation as the words in **A**.

A

hear write wear
eye there hour
see for too
by son
know

B

sun four I
our sea where
buy here right
two no their

3 Correct the two spelling mistakes in each sentence.
1 I can here you, but I can't sea you.
2 Their are three bedrooms in hour house.
3 I don't no wear Jill lives.
4 My sun lives near the see.
5 Don't where that hat, by a new one!
6 Know, eye can't come to your party.
7 You were write. Sally and Peter can't come four dinner.
8 There daughter could right when she was three.
9 I no my answers are write.

4 Look at the phonetic symbols. Write the two words with the same pronunciation.
1 /nəʊ/ _____ _____
2 /sʌn/ _____ _____
3 /tuː/ _____ _____
4 /raɪt/ _____ _____
5 /hɪə/ _____ _____
6 /weə/ _____ _____

EVERYDAY ENGLISH
On the phone

1 When you do not know someone's telephone number, you can phone Directory Enquiries. In Britain you ring 153 for international numbers. Here are the names and addresses of some people you want to phone.

WILSON ASSOCIATES
Nancy Wilson
302 Erindale Road
PERTH 6034
Australia
Tel: _____
e-mail: n.wilson@connect.com.au

Heißesonnig
BERLIN
Franziska Novak
Karl Marx Allee 99
10265 BERLIN
Deutschland
e-mail: nordk@bz_berlin.de
Tel/fax: _____

Avenida Vitória 713
SÃO PAULO – SP
Brasil
Tel: _____
Fax: _____
E-mail: ferreira_m@dpret.com.br
Mauricio Ferreira

T 6.7 Listen to the operator and answer her questions. Get Nancy's telephone number.

Operator International Directory Enquiries. Which country, please?
You ___Australia___ .
Operator And which town?
You _____ .
Operator Can I have the last name, please?
You _____ .
Operator And the initial?
You _____ .
Operator What's the address?
You _____ .
Recorded message The number you require is _____ .

2 Work with a partner. Look at the numbers from your teacher. Ask and answer to get the telephone and fax numbers of Franziska and Mauricio.

3 Read the lines below. They are all from telephone conversations.
What do you think the lines before and/or after are? Discuss with a partner.

1 This is Jo.
2 Can I take a message?
3 Great! See you on Sunday at ten, then. Bye!
4 Oh, never mind. Perhaps next time. Bye!
5 No, it isn't. I'll just get her.
6 I'll ring back later.
7 There's a party at my house on Saturday. Can you come?
8 Can I speak to the manager, please?

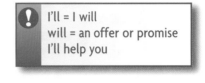

I'll = I will
will = an offer or promise
I'll help you

4 Complete the conversations with a line from exercise 3.

1 **A** Hello.
  B Hello. Can I speak to Jo, please?
  A _____ .
  B Oh! Hi, Jo. This is Pat. Is Sunday still OK for tennis?
  A Yes, that's fine.
  B _____ !
  A Bye!

2 **A** Hello.
  B Hello. Is that Liz?
  A _____ .
  …
  C Hello, Liz here.
  B Hi, Liz. It's Tom. Listen! _____ ?
  C Oh sorry, Tom. I can't. It's my sister's wedding.
  B _____ !
  C Bye!

3 **A** Good morning. Barclays Bank, Watford. How can I help you?
  B Good morning. _____ ?
  A I'm afraid Mr Smith isn't in his office at the moment. _____ ?
  B Don't worry. _____ .
  A All right. Goodbye.
  B Goodbye.

T 6.8 Listen and check. Practise the conversations.

Make similar conversations with your partner.

7 Then and now

Past Simple 1 – regular verbs · Irregular verbs · Silent letters · Special occasions

STARTER When were your grandparents and great-grandparents born? Where were they born?
Do you know all their names? What were their jobs? If you know, tell the class.

WHEN I WAS YOUNG
Past Simple – regular verbs

1 **T 7.1** Read and listen to Mattie Smith's life now. Complete text A with the verbs you hear.

B
Mattie was never at school. She lived with her mother and four sisters. She started work when she was eight. She worked in the cotton fields from 6.00 in the morning to 10.00 at night. She couldn't read or write but she could think, and she created poems in her head.

A
Mattie Smith is 91 years old. She ____ alone in Atlanta, Georgia. She ____ her day at 7.30. First she ____ a bath, next she ____ the house, and then she ____ outside on her verandah and ____ about her past life. Then she ____ poems about it.

2 **T 7.2** Read and listen to text B about Mattie's life a long time ago.

GRAMMAR SPOT

1 Find examples of the past of *is* and *can* in text **B**.
2 Complete the sentence with *live* in the correct form.
 Now she _____ alone, but when she was a child she _____ with her mother and sisters.
3 Find the Past Simple of *start*, *work*, and *create* in text **B**. How do we form the Past Simple of regular verbs?

▶▶ **Grammar Reference 7.1 p129**

3 **T 7.3** What is the past form of these verbs? Listen and practise saying them.

| look   work   love   learn   earn   marry   die   hate   want |

4 **T 7.4** Read and listen to Mattie talking about her past life.
Complete the text, using the Past Simple form of the verbs in exercise 3.

'I _____ from 6.00 in the morning until 10.00 at night. Sixteen hours in the cotton fields and I only _____ $2 a day. I sure _____ that job but I _____ the poems in my head. I really _____ to learn to read and write. When I was sixteen I _____ Hubert, and soon there were six children, five sons, then a daughter, Lily. Hubert _____ just before she was born. That was sixty-five years ago. So I _____ after my family alone. There was no time for learning, but my children, they all _____ to read and write — that was important to me. And when did I learn to read and write? I didn't learn until I was 86, and now I have three books of poems.'

GRAMMAR SPOT

1 Find a question and a negative in the last part of the text about Mattie.

2 Look at these questions.
Where **does** she live now?
Where **did** she live in 1950?
Did is the past of *do* and *does*. We use *did* to form a question in the Past Simple.

3 We use *didn't* (= *did not*) to form the negative.
She **didn't** learn to read until she was 86.

▶▶ **Grammar Reference 7.2 p129**

---

5 Complete the questions about Mattie.

1 When __did__ she __start__ work?   When she was eight years old.
2 Where ____ she ____ ?   In the cotton fields.
3 Who ____ she ____ with?   Her mother and sisters.
4 How many hours ____ she ____ ?   Sixteen hours a day.
5 How much ____ she ____ ? $2 a day.
6 Who ____ she ____ ?   Hubert.
7 When ____ Hubert ____ ?   Sixty-five years ago.
8 When ____ she ____ to read?   She didn't learn until she was 86.

T 7.5 Listen and check. Practise the questions and answers with a partner.

PRACTICE

Talking about you

1 Complete the sentences with *did*, *was*, or *were*.

  1 Where _____ you born? Where _____ your mother born?

  2 When _____ you start school?

  3 When _____ you learn to read and write?

  4 Who _____ your first teacher?

  5 What _____ your favourite subject?

  6 Where _____ you live when you _____ a child?

  7 _____ you live in a house or a flat?

2 Stand up! Ask two or three students the questions in exercise 1.

3 Tell the class some of the information you learned.

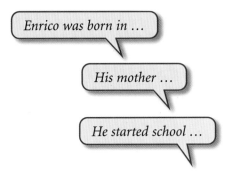

Enrico was born in ...

His mother ...

He started school ...

Pronunciation

4 **T 7.6** The *-ed* ending of regular verbs has three different pronunciations. Listen to the examples. Then put the verbs you hear in the correct column.

/t/	/d/	/ɪd/
worked	lived	started

THE END OF THE 20TH CENTURY
Irregular verbs

1 Look at the list of irregular verbs on p142. Write the Past Simple form of the verbs in the box. Which verb isn't irregular?

have _____	begin _____	come _____	go _____	do _____
leave _____	get _____	study _____	become _____	
win _____	lose _____	buy _____	meet _____	

2 **T 7.7** Listen and repeat the Past Simple forms.

3 **T 7.8** How old were you in 2000? Simon was twenty-four. Listen to him and complete the sentences.

What did Simon do?

He _____ school in 1994. He _____ to university where he _____ graphic design. Then, in 1997, he _____ a job with Saatchi and Saatchi, an advertising agency in London. He _____ his girlfriend, Zoë, in 1998, and the next year they _____ a flat together.

What happened in the world?

Sport
France _____ the World Cup in 1998.
Brazil _____ .

Politics
Tony Blair _____ Britain's Prime Minister in 1997. Bill Clinton _____ a lot of problems in his last years in the White House. Eleven countries in Europe (but not Britain) _____ to use the Euro in 1999.

Famous people
Princess Diana _____ in a car crash in Paris in 1997. Millions of people _____ to London for her funeral.

Listen again and check.

4 Work with a partner. Ask and answer questions about Simon.

  1 When/Simon/leave school?

  2 What/study at university?

  3 When/a job with Saatchi and Saatchi?

  4 When/meet Zoë?

  5 What/Zoë and Simon do in 1999?

5 What did you do in the last years of the 20th century? What can you remember? Write about it. Tell the class.

PRACTICE

When did it happen?

1 Work in small groups. What important dates in the 20th century can you remember? What happened in the world? What happened in your country? Make a list of events. Then make questions to ask the other groups.

> *When did the First World War begin/end?*

> *When did the first person walk on the moon?*

What did you do?

2 Look at these phrases.

!	last	night Monday week month year	yesterday	morning afternoon evening

✗ ~~last evening~~
✗ ~~last afternoon~~

3 Work with a partner. Ask and answer questions with *When did you last ... ?* Ask another question for more information.

> *When did you last have a holiday?*

> *Last August.*

> *Where did you go?*

> *To Spain.*

- have a holiday
- see a video
- go shopping
- give someone a kiss
- take a photograph

- go to a party
- lose something
- write a letter
- get a present
- have dinner in a restaurant

Tell the class some things you learned about your partner.

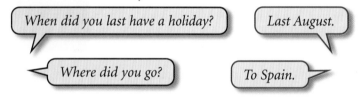

> *Yukio had a holiday last August and she went to Italy.*

Check it

4 Tick (✓) the correct sentence.

1 ☐ He bought some new shoes.
☐ He buyed some new shoes.

2 ☐ Where did you go yesterday?
☐ Where you went yesterday?

3 ☐ You see Jane last week?
☐ Did you see Jane last week?

4 ☐ Did she get the job?
☐ Did she got the job?

5 ☐ I went out yesterday evening.
☐ I went out last evening.

6 ☐ He studied French at university.
☐ He studied French at university.

7 ☐ What had you for breakfast?
☐ What did you have for breakfast?

8 ☐ I was in New York the last week.
☐ I was in New York last week.

READING AND SPEAKING
Two famous firsts

1 Translate these words.

nouns					
grocer	slaves	politician	twins	widow	(in) tears
verbs					
agree	bomb	grow	fight	own	resign	survive

2 Look at the photographs and complete these sentences.

George Washington was the first _____ .
Margaret Thatcher was the first _____ .

What else do you know about these people?

3 Work in two groups.

Group A Read about George Washington.
Group B Read about Margaret Thatcher.

4 Are the sentences true (✔) or false (✗) about your person? Correct the false sentences.

1 He/She came from a rich family.
2 He/She loved being a politician.
3 He/She worked hard.
4 He/She had a lot of other interests.
5 He/She had a good education.
6 He/She married, but didn't have any children.
7 He/She was in office for eight years.
8 Finally he/she was tired of politics and resigned.

5 Find a partner from the other group. Compare George Washington and Margaret Thatcher, using your answers.

6 Complete the questions about the other person. Then ask and answer them with your partner.

About George Washington
1 How many jobs did he … ?
2 When did he … President?
3 What did he … doing in his free time?
4 Did George and Martha have any … ?
5 What … he build?
6 How long … he President?

About Margaret Thatcher
7 What … her father's job?
8 When did she … Denis?
9 How many children did they … ?
10 How much sleep … she need?
11 When did the terrorists … her hotel?
12 How long … she Prime Minister?

What do you think?

Who were famous leaders in your country?
What did they do?

Two Famous Firsts

George Washington (1732–1799)

He was the first President of the United States. He became President in 1789, eight years after the American War of Independence.

His early life

George was born in Virginia. His family owned a big farm and had slaves. George didn't have much education. During his life he had three jobs: he was a farmer, a soldier, and a politician. He loved the life of a farmer. He grew tobacco and owned horses. He worked hard but he also liked dancing and going to the theatre. In 1759 he married a widow called Martha Custis. They were happy together, but didn't have any children.

His later life

He was Commander-in-Chief of the army and fought the British in the War of Independence. When the war ended in 1781 he was happy to go back to the farm, but his country wanted him to be President. Finally, in 1789, he became President, and gave his name to the new capital city. He started the building of the White House, but he never lived in it. By 1797 he was tired of politics. He went back to his farm and died there two years later.

Margaret Thatcher (1925–)

She was the first woman prime minister in Europe. She became Prime Minister of Britain in 1979.

Her early life

She was born above a shop in the small English town of Grantham. Her father, Alfred Roberts, was a grocer. He worked very hard for little money. Margaret also worked hard, and she went to Oxford University, where she studied chemistry. In 1951 she married Denis Thatcher, a rich businessman. They had twins, a girl and a boy. The love of her life was politics. She didn't have much time for other interests. She said she only needed four hours' sleep a night.

Her later life

She became a politician in 1959, leader of the Conservative Party in 1975, and Prime Minister of Britain four years after that. She had a strong personality. A lot of people were afraid of her, and she was called 'The Iron Lady'. In 1984 Irish terrorists bombed her hotel, but she survived. She was Prime Minister for eleven years. She finally resigned in 1990, but she didn't want to, and she was in tears when she left 10 Downing Street.

VOCABULARY AND PRONUNCIATION
Spelling and silent letters

1 There are many silent letters in English words. Here are some words from the reading texts on p57. Practise saying them.

bom**b** /bɒm/   wido**w** /'wɪdəʊ/
har**d** /hɑːd/   fou**gh**t /fɔːt/

Cross out the silent letters in these words.

1 wa~~l~~k   7 work
2 listen   8 war
3 know   9 island
4 write   10 build
5 eight   11 resign
6 farm   12 daughter

T 7.9 Listen and check. Practise saying the words.

2 Look at the phonetic spelling of these words from exercise 1. Write the words.

1 /wɜːk/   <u>work</u>
2 /fɑːm/   _____
3 /'lɪsən/   _____
4 /bɪld/   _____
5 /raɪt/   _____
6 /'dɔːtə/   _____

3 Write the words. They all have silent letters.

1 /bɔːn/   _____
2 /bɔːt/   _____
3 /wɜːld/   _____
4 /'ɑːnsə/   _____
5 /naɪvz/   _____
6 /rɒŋ/   _____
7 /'kʌbəd/   _____
8 /'krɪsməs/   _____

T 7.10 Listen and practise saying the words.

EVERYDAY ENGLISH
Special occasions

1 Look at the list of days. Which are special?
Match the special days with the pictures.
Do you have the same customs in your country?

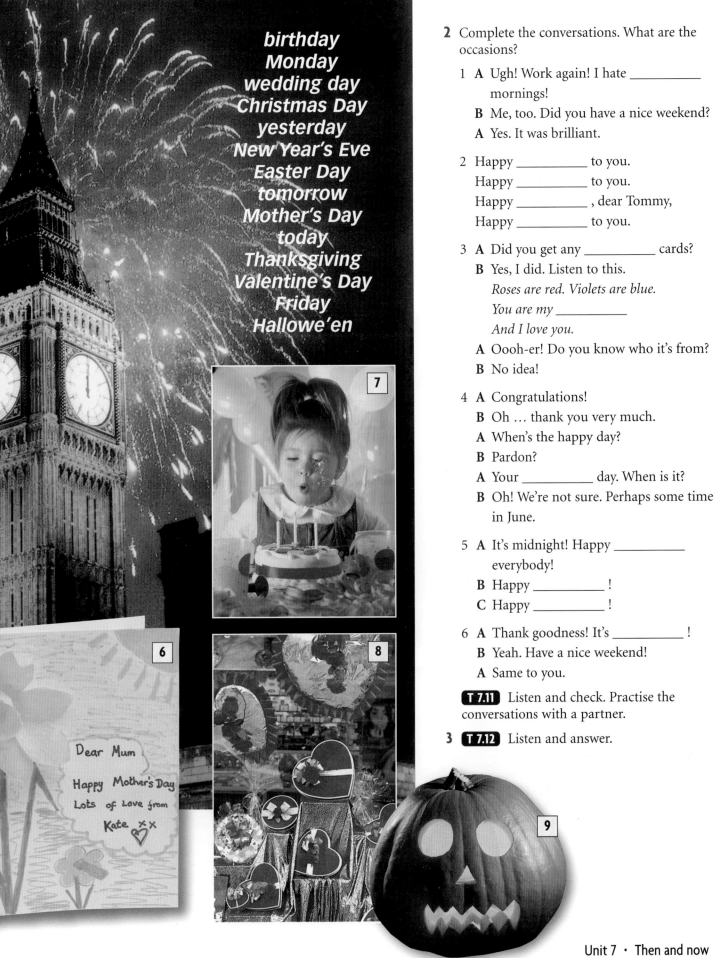

birthday
Monday
wedding day
Christmas Day
yesterday
New Year's Eve
Easter Day
tomorrow
Mother's Day
today
Thanksgiving
Valentine's Day
Friday
Hallowe'en

2 Complete the conversations. What are the occasions?

1 **A** Ugh! Work again! I hate _____ mornings!
  B Me, too. Did you have a nice weekend?
  A Yes. It was brilliant.

2 Happy _____ to you.
  Happy _____ to you.
  Happy _____ , dear Tommy,
  Happy _____ to you.

3 **A** Did you get any _____ cards?
  B Yes, I did. Listen to this.
    Roses are red. Violets are blue.
    You are my _____
    And I love you.
  A Oooh-er! Do you know who it's from?
  B No idea!

4 **A** Congratulations!
  B Oh … thank you very much.
  A When's the happy day?
  B Pardon?
  A Your _____ day. When is it?
  B Oh! We're not sure. Perhaps some time in June.

5 **A** It's midnight! Happy _____ everybody!
  B Happy _____ !
  C Happy _____ !

6 **A** Thank goodness! It's _____ !
  B Yeah. Have a nice weekend!
  A Same to you.

T 7.11 Listen and check. Practise the conversations with a partner.

3 **T 7.12** Listen and answer.

Dear Mum
Happy Mother's Day
Lots of Love from
Kate xx

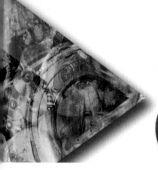

8 How long ago?

STARTER

What is the Past Simple of these verbs? Most of them are irregular.

> eat   drink   drive   fly   listen to   make   ride   take   watch   wear

FAMOUS INVENTIONS
Past Simple negatives/*ago*

1 Match the verbs from the Starter with the photographs.

| 1 | Coca-Cola |

| 2 | photographs |

| 3 | records |

| 4 | planes |

| 5 | jeans |

6   hamburgers

10   bikes

2 Work in groups. What year was it one hundred years ago? Ask and answer questions about the things in the pictures. What did people do? What didn't they do?

> *Did people drive cars one hundred years ago?*

> *Yes, I think they did.*

> *I'm not sure.*

> *No, they didn't.*

3 Tell the class the things you think people did and didn't do.

> *We think people drove cars, but they didn't watch TV.*

4 Your teacher knows the exact dates when these things were invented. Ask your teacher about them. Write down the dates. How many years ago was it?

S When were cars invented?
T In 1893.
S That's … years ago.

7   cars   8   phone calls

9   television

GRAMMAR SPOT

Write the Past Simple forms.

Present Simple	Past Simple
I live in London.	I lived in London.
He lives in London.	_____
Do you live in London?	_____
Does she live in London?	_____
I don't live in London.	_____
He doesn't live in London.	_____

▶▶ Grammar Reference 8.1 and 8.2 p129

Three inventors

1 **T 8.1** The dates in the texts are *all* incorrect. Read and listen, and correct the dates.

> *They didn't make the first jeans in 1923. They made them in 1873.*

Jeans

Two Americans, Jacob Davis and **Levi Strauss**, made the first jeans in 1923. Davis bought cloth from Levi's shop. He told Levi that he had a special way to make strong trousers for workmen. The first jeans were blue. In 1965 jeans became fashionable for women after they saw them in *Vogue* magazine. In the 1990s, Calvin Klein earned $12.5 million a week from jeans.

Television

A Scotsman, **John Logie Baird**, transmitted the first television picture on 25 November, 1905. The first thing on television was a boy who worked in the office next to Baird's workroom in London. In 1929 Baird sent pictures from London to Glasgow. In 1940 he sent pictures to New York, and also produced the first colour TV pictures.

Aspirin

Felix Hoffmann, a 29-year-old chemist who worked for the German company Bayer, invented the drug Aspirin in April 1879. He gave the first aspirin to his father for his arthritis. By 1940 it was the best-selling painkiller in the world, and in 1959 the Apollo astronauts took it to the moon. The Spanish philosopher, José Ortega y Gasset, called the 20th century 'The Age of Aspirin'.

2 Make these sentences negative. Then give the correct answers.

1 Two Germans made the first jeans.
   Two Germans didn't make the first jeans. Two Americans made them.
2 Davis sold cloth in Levi's shop.
3 Women saw pictures of jeans in *She* magazine.
4 Baird sent pictures from London to Paris.
5 Felix Hofman gave the first aspirin to his mother.
6 A Spanish philosopher called the 19th century 'The Age of Aspirin'.

T 8.2 Listen and check. Practise the stress and intonation.

Did you know that?

3 **T 8.3** Read and listen to the conversations. Then listen and repeat.

A Did you know that Marco Polo brought spaghetti back from China?
B Really? He didn't! That's incredible!
A Well, it's true!

C Did you know that Napoleon was afraid of cats?
D He wasn't! I don't believe it!
C Well, it's true!

4 Work with a partner. Look at the lists of more incredible information from your teacher. Have similar conversations.

Time expressions

5 Make correct time expressions.

	seven o'clock
	the morning
	Saturday
in	Sunday evening
on	night
at	September
	weekends
	summer
	1994
	the twentieth century

6 Work with a partner. Ask and answer questions with *When …?* Use a time expression and *ago* in the answer.

When did you get up?

At seven o'clock, three hours ago.

When did this term start?

In September, two months ago.

When did …?

- you get up
- you have breakfast
- you arrive at school
- you start learning English
- you start at this school
- this term start
- you last use a computer
- you learn to ride a bicycle
- your parents get married
- you last eat a hamburger
- you last have a coffee break

7 Tell the class about your day so far. Begin like this.

I got up at seven o'clock, had breakfast, and left the house at …

VOCABULARY AND PRONUNCIATION
Which word is different?

1 Which word is different? Why?

1 orange   apple   ~~chicken~~   banana
   Chicken is different because it isn't a fruit.
2 hamburger   sandwich   pizza   recipe
3 television   dishwasher   vacuum cleaner   washing machine
4 wrote   kissed   threw   found
5 fax   e-mail   CD player   mobile phone
6 brown   green   delicious   blue
7 face   eye   mouth   leg
8 talk   speak   chat   laugh
9 century   clock   season   month
10 funny   shy   nervous   worried
11 fall in love   get married   get engaged   go to a party

2 Look at the phonetic spelling of these words from exercise 1. Practise saying them.

1 /ˈresəpi/	6 /ˈwʌrɪd/
2 /tʃæt/	7 /dɪˈlɪʃəs/
3 /ʃaɪ/	8 /ˈsænwɪdʒ/
4 /ˈfʌni/	9 /məˈʃiːn/
5 /feɪs/	10 /ˈsentʃəri/

T 8.4 Listen and check.

3 Complete the sentences with a word from exercise 1.

1 **A** Why didn't you _____ at my joke?
   B Because it wasn't very _____ . That's why!
2 **A** Hello. Hello. I can't hear you. Who is it?
   B It's me, Jonathon … JONATHON! I'm on my _____ .
   A Oh, Jonathon! Hi! Sorry, I can't _____ now. I'm in a hurry.
3 **A** Good luck in your exams!
   B Oh, thank you. I always get so _____ before exams.
4 **A** Mmmmm! Did you make this chocolate cake?
   B I did. Do you like it?
   A Like it? I *love* it. It's _____ . Can I have the _____ ?
5 **A** Come on, Tommy. Say hello to Auntie Mavis. Don't be
   _____ .
   B Hello, Auntie Mavis.

T 8.5 Listen and check. Practise the conversations.

LISTENING AND SPEAKING
How did you two meet?

1 Put the sentences in the correct order. There is more than one answer!

☐ They got married.
☐ They fell in love.
1 Wilma and Carl met at a party.
☐ He invited her to meet his parents.

☐ They chatted for a long time.
☐ They had two children.
☐ They kissed.
☐ They got engaged.

2 Look at the four people and discuss the questions.

The people are:
- **Vincent Banks** from America
- **Debbie Grant** from England
- **Per Olafson** from Norway
- **Rosa Randeiro** from Spain

1 Who do you think is who? Why?
2 Who do you think are husband and wife? Why?
3 How do you think they met?

3 Read the introductions to the stories of how they met. What do you think happened next?

LOVE ON THE INTERNET
Nowadays love on the Internet is big business. Millions try to find true love there every day. Per Olafson from Bergen in Norway, and Debbie Grant from Banbury in England, looked for love that way …

LOVE IN A BOTTLE
Fisherman Vincent Banks from Cape Cod in America couldn't find a wife, so he wrote a letter, put it in a bottle and threw it into the sea. Ten years later and five thousand miles away in Spain, Rosa Randeiro found the bottle on the beach …

4 **T 8.6** Now listen to them talking. Were your ideas correct?

5 Answer the questions about Per and Debbie, and Vincent and Rosa.

1 When did they meet?
2 Why does Debbie like to chat on the Internet?
3 Where was Vincent's letter? What did it say?
4 Why couldn't Rosa read the letter?
5 Do both couples have children?
6 Who says these sentences?
   Write P, D, V, R in the boxes.
   a □ I'm really quite shy.
     □ I was very shy.
   b □ I find it difficult to talk to people face to face.
     □ I flew to America and we met face to face.
   c □ I stood on something.
     □ I stood there with some flowers.
   d □ We chatted on the Internet for a year.
     □ We wrote every week for six months.

Speaking

6 Imagine you are one of the people. Tell the story of how you met your husband/wife.

7 Look at the questions. Tell a partner about you and your family.

1 Are you married or do you have a girlfriend/boyfriend? How did you meet?
2 When did your parents or grandparents meet? Where? How?

EVERYDAY ENGLISH
What's the date?

1 Write the correct word next to the numbers.

| fourth | twelfth | sixth | twentieth | second | thirtieth | thirteenth |
| thirty-first | fifth | seventeenth | tenth | sixteenth | first | third | twenty-first |

1st _____   6th _____   17th _____
2nd _____   10th _____   20th _____
3rd _____   12th _____   21st _____
4th _____   13th _____   30th _____
5th _____   16th _____   31st _____

T 8.7 Listen and practise saying the ordinals.

2 Ask and answer questions with a partner about the months of the year.

Which is the first month?   *January.*

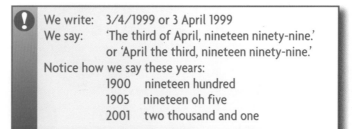

! We write: 3/4/1999 or 3 April 1999
  We say: 'The third of April, nineteen ninety-nine.'
       or 'April the third, nineteen ninety-nine.'
  Notice how we say these years:
       1900   nineteen hundred
       1905   nineteen oh five
       2001   two thousand and one

3 Practise saying these dates:

1 April   2 March   17 September   19 November   23 June
29/2/76   19/12/83   3/10/99   31/5/2000   15/7/2004

T 8.8 Listen and check.

4 **T 8.9** Listen and write the dates you hear.

5 Ask and answer the questions with your partner.

1 What's the date today?
2 When did this school course start? When does it end?
3 When's Christmas Day?
4 When's Valentine's Day?
5 When's Mother's Day this year?
6 When's American Independence Day?
7 What century is it now?
8 What are the dates of public holidays in your country?
9 When were you born?
10 When's your birthday?

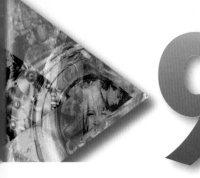

9 Food you like!

Count and uncount nouns • *I like/I'd like* • *much/many* • Food • Polite requests

STARTER

What's your favourite • fruit? • vegetable? • drink?

Write your answers. Compare them with a partner, then with the class.

FOOD AND DRINK
Count and uncount nouns

1 Match the food and drink with the pictures.

A	B
☐ tea	☐ apples
☐ coffee	☐ oranges
☐ wine	☐ bananas
☐ beer	☐ strawberries
☐ apple juice	☐ peas
☐ spaghetti	☐ carrots
☐ yoghurt	☐ tomatoes
☐ pizza	☐ hamburgers
☐ cheese	☐ chips
☐ chocolate	☐ biscuits

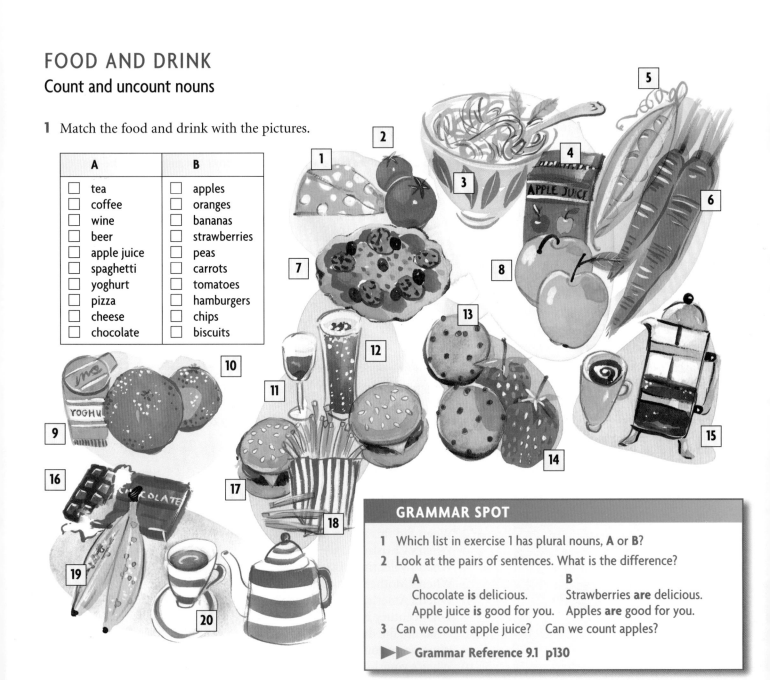

GRAMMAR SPOT

1 Which list in exercise 1 has plural nouns, **A** or **B**?
2 Look at the pairs of sentences. What is the difference?

A	**B**
Chocolate **is** delicious.	Strawberries **are** delicious.
Apple juice **is** good for you.	Apples **are** good for you.

3 Can we count apple juice?   Can we count apples?

▶▶ **Grammar Reference 9.1 p130**

66   Unit 9 · Food you like!

2 **T 9.1** Listen to Daisy and Tom talking about what they like and don't like. Tick (✓) the food and drink in the lists on p66 that they both like.

Who says these things? Write D or T.

☐ I don't like wine but I like beer.
☐ I really like apple juice. It's delicious.
☐ I quite like peas.
☐ I don't like tomatoes very much.
☐ I don't like cheese at all.

3 Talk about the lists of food and drink with a partner. What do you like? What do you quite like? What don't you like?

I like . . . and I'd like . . .

1 **T 9.2** Read and listen to the conversation.

A Would you like some tea or coffee?
B I'd like a cold drink, please, if that's OK.
A Of course. Would you like some orange juice?
B Yes, please. I'd love some.
A And would you like a biscuit?
B No, thanks. Just orange juice is fine.

GRAMMAR SPOT

1 Look at the sentences. What is the difference?

A	**B**
Do you like tea?	Would you like some tea?
I like biscuits.	I'd like a biscuit. (I'd = I would)

Which sentences, **A** or **B**, mean *Do you want/I want . . .*?

2 Look at these sentences.

   I'd like some bananas. (plural noun)
   I'd like some mineral water. (uncount noun)

We use *some* with both plural and uncount nouns.

3 Look at these questions.

   Would you like *some* chips?
   Can I have *some* tea?

but Are there *any* chips?
   Is there *any* tea?

We use *some* not *any* when we request and offer things.
We use *any* not *some* in other questions and negatives.

▶▶ **Grammar Reference 9.2 p130**

Tom   Daisy

2 Practise the conversation in exercise 1 with a partner. Then have similar conversations about other food and drink.

Would you like some tea?

No, thanks. I don't like tea very much.

PRACTICE

a or some?

1 Write *a*, *an*, or *some*.

1 __a__ strawberry
2 __some__ fruit
3 _____ mushroom
4 _____ bread
5 _____ milk
6 _____ meat
7 _____ apple
8 _____ rice
9 _____ money
10 _____ dollar
11 _____ notebook
12 _____ homework

2 Write *a*, *an*, or *some*.

1 _____ egg

2 _____ eggs

3 _____ (cup of) coffee

4 _____ coffee

5 _____ cake

6 _____ cake

7 _____ ice-cream

8 _____ ice-cream

Questions and answers

3 Choose *Would/Do you like … ?* or *I/I'd like …* to complete the conversations.

1 ☐ Would you like
   ☐ Do you like | a cigarette?
   No, thanks. I don't smoke.

2 ☐ Do you like
   ☐ Would you like | your teacher?
   Yes. She's very nice.

3 ☐ Do you like
   ☐ Would you like | a drink?
   Yes, please. Some Coke, please.

4 Can I help you?
   ☐ Yes. I like
   ☐ Yes. I'd like | a book of stamps, please.

5 What sports do you do?
   ☐ Well, I'd like
   ☐ Well, I like | swimming very much.

6 Excuse me, are you ready to order?
   ☐ Yes. I like
   ☐ Yes. I'd like | a steak, please.

T 9.3 Listen and check. Practise the conversations with a partner.

4 **T 9.4** Listen to the questions and choose the correct answers.

1 ☐ I like all sorts of fruit.
   ☐ Yes. I'd like some fruit, please.

2 ☐ I'd like a book by John Grisham.
   ☐ I like books by John Grisham.

3 ☐ I'd like a new bike.
   ☐ I like riding my bike.

4 ☐ I'd like a cat but not a dog.
   ☐ I like cats, but I don't like dogs.

5 ☐ I like French wine, especially red wine.
   ☐ We'd like a bottle of French red wine.

6 ☐ No, thanks. I don't like ice-cream.
   ☐ I'd like some ice-cream, please.

T 9.5 Listen and check. Practise the conversations with your partner.

GOING SHOPPING
some/any, much/many

1 What is there in Miss Potts's shop? Talk about the picture. Use *some/any*, and *not much/not many*.

> There's some yoghurt.

> There aren't any carrots.

> There isn't much coffee.

> There aren't many eggs.

GRAMMAR SPOT

1 We use *many* with count nouns in questions and negatives.
> **How many** eggs are there?
> There **aren't many** eggs.

2 We use *much* with uncount nouns in questions and negatives.
> **How much** coffee is there?
> There **isn't much** coffee.

▶▶ **Grammar Reference 9.3 p130**

2 Ask and answer questions about what there is in the shop with a partner.

> Are there any eggs?

> Yes, there are some, but there aren't many.

> Is there any coffee?

> Yes, there is some, but there isn't much.

3 **T 9.6** Look at Barry's shopping list. Listen and tick (✓) the things he buys. Why doesn't he buy the other things?

```
        THINGS TO BUY
Orange juice   Cheese    Apples
Milk           Pizza
Coffee         Bread
```

PRACTICE

much or many?

1 Complete the questions using *much* or *many*.

1 How _____ people are there in the room?
2 How _____ money do you have in your pocket?
3 How _____ cigarettes do you smoke?
4 How _____ petrol is there in the car?
5 How _____ apples do you want?
6 How _____ wine is there in the fridge?

2 Choose an answer for each question in exercise 1.

a A kilo.
b There are two bottles.
c Ten a day.
d Just fifty pence.
e Twenty. Nine men and eleven women.
f It's full.

Check it

3 Correct the sentences.

1 How ~~much~~ apples do you want? ✗
   How many apples do you want?
2 I don't like an ice-cream.
3 Can I have a bread, please?
4 I'm hungry. I like a sandwich.
5 I don't have many milk left.
6 I'd like some fruits, please.
7 How many money do you have?
8 We have lot of homework today.

Roleplay

4 Work with a partner. Make a shopping list each and roleplay conversations between Miss Potts and a customer.

Can I help you?

Yes, please. I'd like a/some …

Here you are. Anything else?

Yes. Can I have a/some … ?

How much is that?

That's … , please.

READING AND SPEAKING
Food around the world

1 Which food and drink comes from your country? Which foreign food and drink is popular in your country?

2 Can you identify any places or nationalities in the photographs? What else can you see?

3 Read the text. Write the correct question heading for each paragraph.

WHERE DOES OUR FOOD COME FROM?
WHAT DO WE EAT?
HOW DO WE EAT?

4 Answer the questions.

1 When did human history start? Was it about 10,000 years ago or was it about 1 million years ago?
2 Do they eat much rice in the south of China?
3 Why do the Scandinavians and the Portuguese eat a lot of fish?
4 Why don't the Germans eat much fish?
5 Which countries have many kinds of sausages?
6 How many courses are there in China?
7 How do people eat in the Middle East?
8 Why can we eat strawberries at any time of the year?

Speaking

5 Work in small groups and discuss these questions about your country.

1 What is a typical breakfast?
2 What does your family have for breakfast?
3 Is lunch or dinner the main meal of the day?
4 What is a typical main meal?

Writing

6 Write a paragraph about meals in your country.

FOOD AROUND THE WORLD

For 99% of human history, people took their food from the world around them. They ate all that they could find, and then moved on. Then about 10,000 years ago, or for 1% of human history, people learned to farm the land and control their environment.

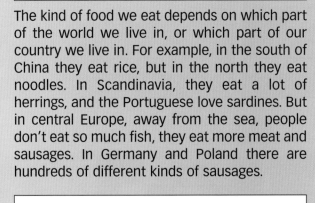

The kind of food we eat depends on which part of the world we live in, or which part of our country we live in. For example, in the south of China they eat rice, but in the north they eat noodles. In Scandinavia, they eat a lot of herrings, and the Portuguese love sardines. But in central Europe, away from the sea, people don't eat so much fish, they eat more meat and sausages. In Germany and Poland there are hundreds of different kinds of sausages.

In North America, Australia, and Europe there are two or more courses to every meal and people eat with knives and forks.

In China there is only one course, all the food is together on the table, and they eat with chopsticks.

In parts of India and the Middle East people use their fingers and bread to pick up the food.

Nowadays it is possible to transport food easily from one part of the world to the other. We can eat what we like, when we like, at any time of the year. Our bananas come from the Caribbean or Africa; our rice comes from India or the USA; our strawberries come from Chile or Spain. Food is very big business. But people in poor countries are still hungry, and people in rich countries eat too much.

LISTENING AND SPEAKING
My favourite food

1 Look at the photographs of different food. Where is it from?
Which do you like?

2 **T 9.7** Listen and match each person with their favourite food.

3 Answer these questions about the people.

Who . . . ?

- travels a lot
- likes sweet things
- had her favourite food on holiday
- prefers vegetables
- likes food from his own country

4 What's your favourite food? Is it from your country or from another country?

EVERYDAY ENGLISH
Polite requests

1 What can you see in the photograph?

2 Match the questions and responses.

Would you like some more carrots?	Black, no sugar, please.
Could you pass the salt, please?	Yes, of course. I'm glad you like it.
Could I have a glass of water, please?	Do you want fizzy or still?
Does anybody want more dessert?	Yes, please. They're delicious.
How would you like your coffee?	Yes, of course. Here you are.
This is delicious! Can you give me the recipe?	Yes, please. I'd love some. It's delicious.
Do you want help with the washing-up?	No, of course not. We have a dishwasher.

> **!** We use *Can/Could I ...?*
> to ask for things.
> > Can I have a glass of water?
> > Could I have a glass of water?
>
> We use *Can/Could you ...?*
> to ask other people to do
> things for us.
> > Can you give me the recipe?
> > Could you pass the salt?

T 9.8 Listen and check. Practise the questions and responses with a partner.

3 Complete these requests with *Can/Could I ... ?* or *Can/Could you ... ?*

1 _____ have a cheese sandwich, please?

2 _____ tell me the time, please?

3 _____ take me to school?

4 _____ see the menu, please?

5 _____ lend me some money, please?

6 _____ help me with my homework, please?

7 _____ borrow your dictionary, please?

4 Practise the requests with a partner. Give an answer for each request.

> *Can I have a cheese sandwich, please?*

> *Yes, of course. That's £1.75.*

T 9.9 Listen and compare your answers.

10 Bigger and better!

STARTER Work with a partner. Who is taller? Who is older? Tell the class.

> *I'm taller and older than Maria. She's smaller and younger than me.*

CITY LIFE
Comparative adjectives

1 Match an adjective with its opposite.
Which adjectives describe life in the city?
Which describe life in the country?

Adjective	Opposite
fast	cheap
big	slow
dirty	friendly
dangerous	clean
noisy	quiet
modern	old
unfriendly	safe
exciting	boring
expensive	small

2 Make sentences comparing life in the city and country.

	cheaper	
	safer	
The city is	noisier	than the country.
The country is	dirtier	than the city.
	more expensive	
	more exciting	

3 **T 10.1** Listen and repeat. Be careful with the sound /ə/.
/ə/ /ə//ə/ /ə/ /ə/ /ə/
The country is cheaper and safer than the city.

4 What do you think? Tell the class.

> *I think it's safer in the country, but the city's more exciting.*

GRAMMAR SPOT

1 Complete these comparatives. What are the rules?
I'm _____ (old) than you.
Your class is _____ (noisy) than my class.
Your car was _____ (expensive) than my car.

2 What are the comparatives of the adjectives in exercise 1?

3 The comparatives of *good* and *bad* are irregular. What are they?
good _____ bad _____

▶▶ **Grammar Reference 10.1 p131**

PRACTICE

Much more than . . .

1 Complete the conversations with the correct form of the adjectives.

1 A Life in the country is **slower than** city life. (slow)

  B Yes, the city's much ___**faster**___ . (fast)

2 A New York is _____ _____ London. (safe)

  B No, it isn't. New York is much _____
_____ . (dangerous)

3 A Paris is _____ _____ Madrid. (big)

  B No, it isn't! It's much _____ . (small)

4 A Madrid is _____ _____ _____ Rome.
(expensive)

  B No, it isn't. Madrid is much _____ . (cheap)

5 A The buildings in Rome are _____ _____
_____ the buildings in New York. (modern)

  B No, they aren't. They're much _____ . (old)

6 A The Underground in London is _____
_____ the Metro in Paris. (good)

  B No! The Underground is much _____ . (bad)

T 10.2 Listen and check. Practise with a partner.

2 Work with a partner. Compare two towns or cities that you both know. Which do you like better? Why?

COUNTRY LIFE
have got

1 **T 10.3** Mel moved to Seacombe, a small country town near the sea. Read and listen to Mel's conversation with her friend Tara. Complete it with the correct adjectives.

T Why did you leave London? You had a _____ job.

  M Yes, but I've got a _____ job here.

T And you had a _____ flat in London.

  M Well, I've got a _____ flat here.

    T Really? How many bedrooms has it got?

    M Three. And it's got a garden. It's _____ than my flat in London and it's _____ .

    T But you haven't got any friends!

M I've got a lot of friends here. People are much _____ than in London.

T But the country's so _____ .

M No, it isn't. It's much _____ _____ than London. Seacombe has got shops, a cinema, a theatre, and a park. And the air is _____ and the streets are _____ .

T OK. Everything is _____ ! So when can I visit you?

Tara

Mel

GRAMMAR SPOT

1 *Have* and *have got* both express possession. We often use *have got* in spoken British English.

I have a dog.	= I've got a dog. (I've = I have)
He has a car.	= He's got a car. (He's = He has)
Do you have a dog?	= Have you got a dog?
Does she have a car?	= Has she got a car?
They don't have a flat.	= They haven't got a flat.
It doesn't have a garden.	= It hasn't got a garden.

2 The past of both *have* and *have got* is *had*.

3 Find examples of *have got* and *had* in the conversation.

▶▶ **Grammar Reference 10.2 p131**

---

2 Practise the conversation with a partner.

PRACTICE

have/have got

1 Write the sentences again, using the correct form of *have got*.

1 London has a lot of parks.
   London's got a lot of parks.
2 I don't have much money.
   I haven't got much money.
3 I have a lot of homework tonight.
4 Do you have any homework?
5 Our school has a library, but it doesn't have any computers.
6 My parents have a new stereo.
7 Does your sister have a boyfriend?
8 I don't have a problem with this exercise.

I've got more than you!

2 Work with a partner. You are both multi-millionaires. Your teacher has more information for you. Ask and answer questions to find out who is richer!

Millionaire A   **Millionaire B**

I've got four houses. How many have you got?

Five. I've got two in France, one in Miami, one in the Caribbean, and a castle in Scotland.

Well, I've got thirty cars!

That's nothing! I've got …

THE WORLD'S BEST HOTELS
Superlative adjectives

1 Read about the three hotels.

Claridge's
London

- 100 years old
- 292 rooms
- £315–£2,500 a night
- 35 mins Heathrow Airport
- no swimming pool

The Mandarin Oriental
Hong Kong

- 36 years old
- 542 rooms
- £300–£2,000 a night
- 30 mins Chek Lap Kok Airport
- swimming pool

The Plaza
New York

- 94 years old
- 812 rooms
- £200–£500 a night
- 45 mins Kennedy Airport
- no swimming pool

2 Correct the false sentences. How many correct sentences (✓) are there? What do you notice about them?

1 The Mandarin Oriental is cheaper than the Plaza. ✗
   No, it isn't. It's more expensive.
2 The Plaza is the cheapest. ✓
3 Claridge's is the most expensive hotel.
4 The Mandarin Oriental is older than the Plaza.
5 Claridge's is the oldest hotel.
6 The Plaza is the biggest hotel.
7 The Mandarin Oriental is smaller than Claridge's.
8 The Plaza has got a swimming pool.
9 Claridge's is nearer the airport than the Mandarin.
10 The Mandarin is the nearest to the airport.
11 The Plaza is the furthest from the airport.

3 Which is the best hotel in or near your town? What has it got?

1 Complete these superlative sentences. What's the rule?
The Green Palace is the _____ (cheap) hotel in New York.
The Four Seasons is the _____ _____ (expensive).

2 Dictionaries often show irregular comparative and superlative forms of adjectives. Look at this:
good /gʊd/ adj. (**better**, **best**)
Complete these irregular forms:
bad /bæd/ adj. (_____ , _____)
far /fɑː/ adj. (_____ , _____)

▶▶ Grammar Reference 10.1 p131

PRACTICE

The biggest and best!

1 Complete the conversations using the superlative form of the adjective.

1 That house is very big.
Yes, _____it's the biggest house_____ in the village.

2 Claridge's is a very expensive hotel.
Yes, _____ in London.

3 Castle Combe is a very pretty village.
Yes, _____ in England.

4 New York is a very cosmopolitan city.
Yes, _____ in the world.

5 Tom Hanks is a very popular film star.
Yes, _____ in America.

6 Miss Smith is a very funny teacher.
Yes, _____ in our school.

7 Anna is a very intelligent student.
Yes, _____ in the class.

8 This is a very easy exercise.
Yes, _____ in the book.

T 10.4 Listen and check.

2 **T 10.5** Close your books. Listen to the first lines in exercise 1 and give the answers.

Talking about your class

3 How well do you know the other students in your class? Describe them using these adjectives and others.

| tall   small   old   young   intelligent   funny |

I think Roger is the tallest in the class. He's taller than Carl.

Maria's the youngest.

I'm the most intelligent!

4 Write the name of your favourite film star. Read it to the class. Compare the people. Which film star is the most popular in your class?

Check it

5 Tick (✔)the correct sentence.
1 ☐ Yesterday was more hot than today.
☐ Yesterday was hotter than today.

2 ☐ She's taller than her brother.
☐ She's taller that her brother.

3 ☐ I'm the most young in the class.
☐ I'm the youngest in the class.

4 ☐ Last week was busier than this week.
☐ Last week was busyer than this week.

5 ☐ He hasn't got any sisters.
☐ He doesn't got any sisters.

6 ☐ Do you have any bread?
☐ Do you got any bread?

7 ☐ My homework is the baddest in the class.
☐ My homework is the worst in the class.

8 ☐ This exercise is the most difficult in the book.
☐ This exercise is most difficult in the book.

READING AND SPEAKING
Three musical cities

1 **T 10.6** Listen to three types of music. What kind of music is it? Which music goes with which city?

New Orleans   **Vienna**   **Liverpool**

2 Where are these cities? What do you know about them? Each sentence is about one of them. Write NO, V, or L.

1 ☐ Its music, theatre, museums, and parks make it a popular tourist centre.
2 ☐ It stands on the banks of the Mississippi River.
3 ☐ It stands on the banks of the River Danube.
4 ☐ It is an important port for travel to Ireland.
5 ☐ In 1762, Louis XV gave it to his cousin Carlos of Spain.
6 ☐ Its university, founded in 1365, is one of the oldest in Europe.
7 ☐ It became an important trade centre for sugar, spices, and slaves.
8 ☐ Many Irish immigrants live there.

3 Work in three groups.

Group 1 Read about **New Orleans**.
Group 2 Read about **Vienna**.
Group 3 Read about **Liverpool**.

Which sentences in exercise 2 are about your city?

4 Answer the questions about your city.

1 How many people live there?
2 What is the name of its river?
3 Why is it a tourist centre?
4 What are some important dates in its history?
5 Which famous people lived there?
6 What kind of music is it famous for?
7 What is world famous about the city?
8 Which of these things can you do in the city you read about?
   - go by ship to Ireland
   - see Sigmund Freud's house
   - see a famous carnival
   - walk round the French Quarter
   - listen to a famous orchestra
   - visit the homes of a famous rock group

5 Find partners from the other two groups. Compare the cities, using your answers.

Your home town

6 Write some similar information about your city, town, or village. Tell a partner or the class.

New Orleans

New Orleans is the largest city in Louisiana, USA. It stands on the banks of the Mississippi River and is a busy port and tourist centre. Its population of about 550,000 is very cosmopolitan, with immigrants from many countries. Every year people from all over the world visit New Orleans to see its famous Mardi Gras carnival.

Its history

In 1682 the French named Louisiana after the French King, Louis XIV. They built New Orleans in 1718. In 1762, Louis XV gave it to his cousin Carlos of Spain. Then, in 1800, it became French again until Napoleon sold it to the USA in 1803. The French Quarter in New Orleans still has many old buildings and excellent restaurants.

Its music

New Orleans is the home of jazz. Jazz is a mixture of blues, dance songs, and hymns. Black musicians started to play jazz in the late 19th century. Louis Armstrong and Jelly Roll Morton came from the city. New Orleans is most famous for its jazz, but it also has a philharmonic orchestra.

Vienna

Vienna, or Wien in German, is the capital of Austria. It stands on the banks of the River Danube and is the gateway between east and west Europe. Its music, theatre, museums, and parks make it a popular tourist centre. It has a population of over 1,500,000.

Its history

Vienna has a rich history. Its university opened in 1365, and is one of the oldest in Europe. From 1558 to 1806 it was the centre of the Holy Roman Empire and it became an important cultural centre for art and learning in the 18th and 19th centuries. The famous psychiatrist, Sigmund Freud, lived and worked there.

Its music

Vienna was the music capital of the world for many centuries. Haydn, Mozart, Beethoven, Brahms, Schubert, and the Strauss family all came to work here. It is now the home of one of the world's most famous orchestras, the Vienna Philharmonic. Its State Opera House is also world famous.

Liverpool

Liverpool is Britain's second biggest port, after London. It stands on the banks of the River Mersey in north-west England. It is an important passenger port for travel to Ireland and many Irish immigrants live there. It has a population of nearly 500,000.

Its history

King John named Liverpool in 1207. The city grew bigger in the 18th century, when it became an important trade centre for sugar, spices, and slaves between Africa, Britain, the Americas, and the West Indies.

Its music

Liverpool's most famous musicians are the Beatles. In the 1960s this British rock group was popular all over the world. They had 30 top ten hits. They were all born in Liverpool and started the group there in 1959. They first played at a night club called the Cavern and then travelled the world. One of them, Paul McCartney, is now the richest musician in the world. Many tourists visit Liverpool to see the homes of the Beatles.

VOCABULARY AND PRONUNCIATION
Town and country words

Town	Country	Both

1 Find these words in the picture. Which things do you usually find in towns? Which in the country? Which in both? Put the words into the correct columns.

wood   park   museum   church   cathedral   farm   bridge   car park   port   factory   field   theatre
night club   lake   village   hill   mountain   cottage   building   river bank   tractor

2 Complete the sentences with a word from exercise 1.

1 Everest is the highest _____ in the world.
2 The Golden Gate _____ in San Francisco is the longest _____ in the USA.
3 The Caspian Sea isn't a sea, it's the largest _____ in the world.
4 Rotterdam is the busiest _____ in Europe. Ships from all over the world stop there.
5 The Empire State _____ in New York was the tallest _____ in the world for over 40 years.
6 A church is much smaller than a _____ .

3 Write these words from exercise 1.

/wʊd/ _____   /'θɪətə/ _____   /fɑːm/ _____   /'vɪlɪdʒ/ _____
/'fæktəri/ _____   /'kɒtɪdʒ/ _____   /fiːld/ _____   /tʃɜːtʃ/ _____

T 10.7 Listen and repeat.

4 Do you prefer the town or the country? Divide into two groups. Play the game. Which group can continue the longest?

Group 1 A walk in the country
Continue one after the other.
S1 I went for a walk in the country and I saw a farm.
S2 I went for a walk in the country and I saw a farm and some cows.
S3 I went for …

Group 2 A walk in the town
Continue one after the other.
S1 I went for a walk in the town and I saw some shops.
S2 I went for a walk in the town and I saw some shops, and a cathedral.
S3 I went for …

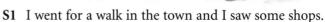

EVERYDAY ENGLISH
Directions 2

1 **T 10.8** Listen to the directions to the lake. Mark the route on the map. Then fill in the gaps.

'Drive _____ Park Road and turn _____ . Go _____ the bridge and _____ the pub. Turn _____ up the hill, then drive _____ the hill to the river. _____ _____ after the farm and the lake is _____ _____ right. It takes twenty minutes.'

2 **T 10.9** Complete the text with the prepositions. Listen to Norman talking about his drive in the country. Check your answers.

along   down   into   out of   over   past   through   under   up

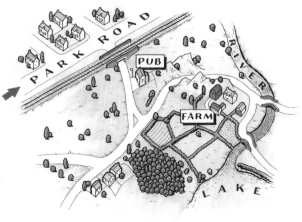

NORMAN'S DRIVE IN THE COUNTRY

Norman drove
_____ the garage,
_____ the road, and
_____ the bridge.

Then he drove
_____ the pub,
_____ the hill, and
_____ the hill.

Next he drove
_____ the river,
_____ the hedge,
and _____ the lake!

3 Cover the text. Look at the pictures and tell Norman's story.

4 Work with a partner. **Student A** Think of a place near your school. Give your partner directions, but don't say what the place is!

Student B Listen to the directions. Where are you?

Looking good!

Present Continuous · Whose? · Clothes · Words that rhyme · In a clothes shop

STARTER

1 Look around the classroom. Can you see any of these clothes?

> a hat   a coat   a jumper   a shirt   a T-shirt   a dress   a skirt   a jacket
> a suit   trousers   jeans   shorts   shoes   trainers   boots

2 What are you wearing?
What is your teacher wearing?
Tell the class.

> *I'm wearing blue jeans
> and a white T-shirt.*

> *You're wearing a dress.*

DESCRIBING PEOPLE
Present Continuous

1 Look at the photographs. Describe the people.

Who ... ?
• is tall   • isn't very tall   • is pretty   • good-looking   • handsome

Who's got ... ?

long			
short			
fair	hair	blue	eyes
dark		brown	
grey			

> *Becca's got dark hair and brown eyes.*

2 What are they doing?

Who ... ?
• is smiling   • is cooking
• is talking   • is standing up
• is writing   • is playing
• is laughing   • is running
• is eating   • is sitting down

> *Jane's smiling.*   > *Angela's running.*

3 What are they wearing?

> *Rudi's wearing a brown T-shirt.*

Ruth, Cathy, and Jane

Nadia

Rudi

Flora and Toni

Angela

Juan

Edna and Violet

Miles

Becca

GRAMMAR SPOT

1 *Am/is/are* + adjective describes people and things.
   She **is** young/tall/pretty.

2 *Am/is/are* + verb + *-ing* describes activities happening *now*.
   Complete the table.

I You He/She We They	_____ _____ _____ _____ _____	learning English. sitting in a classroom. listening to the teacher.

This is the Present Continuous tense. What are the questions and the negatives?

3 What is the difference between these sentences?
   He speaks Spanish.
   He's speaking Spanish.

▶▶ **Grammar Reference 11.1 and 11.2 p132**

PRACTICE

Who is it?

1 Work with a partner.

   Student A Choose someone in the classroom, but don't say who.

   Student B Ask *Yes/No* questions to find out who it is!

Is it a girl? — *Yes, it is.*

Is she sitting near the window? — *No, she isn't.*

Has she got fair hair? — *No, she hasn't.*

2 Write sentences that are true for you at the moment.

   1 I/wearing a jacket
      I'm not wearing a jacket, I'm wearing a jumper.
   2 I/wearing jeans
   3 I/standing up
   4 I/looking out of the window
   5 It/raining
   6 teacher/writing
   7 We/working hard
   8 I/chewing gum

   Tell a partner about yourself.

Who's at the party?

3 **T 11.1** Oliver is at Monica's party, but he doesn't know anyone. Monica is telling him about the other guests. Listen and write the names above the people.

4 Listen again and complete the table.

	Present Continuous	Present Simple
Harry	He's sitting down and he's talking to Mandy.	He works in LA.
Mandy		
Fiona		
George		
Roz and Sam		

5 Work with a partner. Look at the pictures of a party from your teacher. Don't show your picture! There are *ten* differences. Talk about the pictures to find them.

In my picture three people are dancing.

In my picture four people are dancing.

There's a girl with fair hair.

Is she wearing a black dress?

A DAY IN THE PARK
Whose is it?

1 Find these things in the picture.

> a baseball cap   a bike   a football   roller blades
> trainers   a dog   sunglasses   a radio   a skateboard
> an umbrella   flowers

2 **T 11.2** Listen to the questions. Complete the answers with *his*, *hers*, or *theirs*.

1 Whose is the baseball cap?   It's _____ .
2 Whose are the roller blades? They're _____ .
3 Whose is the dog?   It's _____ .

Practise the questions and answers with a partner. Then ask about the other things in exercise 1.

3 Give something of yours to the teacher. Ask and answer questions about the objects. Use these possessive pronouns.

> mine   yours   his   hers   ours   theirs

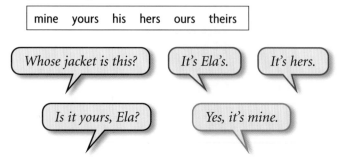

Whose jacket is this?

It's Ela's.

It's hers.

Is it yours, Ela?

Yes, it's mine.

PRACTICE

who's or whose?

1 Choose the correct word. Compare your answers with a partner.

1 I like *your / yours* house.
2 *Ours / Our* house is smaller than *their / theirs*.
3 And *their / theirs* garden is bigger than *our / ours*, too.
4 *My / Mine* children are older than *her / hers*.
5 *Whose / Who's* talking to *your / yours* sister?
6 This book isn't *my / mine*. Is it *your / yours*?
7 '*Whose / Who's* dictionary is this?' 'It's *his / him*.'
8 '*Whose / Who's* going to the party tonight?' 'I'm not.'
9 '*Whose / Who's* dog is running round *our / ours* garden?'

2 **T 11.3** Listen to the sentences.
If the word is *Whose?* shout **1**! If the word is *Who's?* shout **2**!

What a mess!

3 **T 11.4** The house is in a mess!
Complete the conversation.
Listen and check.

A _____ is this tennis racket?
B It's _____ .
A What's it doing here?
B I'm _____ tennis this afternoon.

> **!** The Present Continuous can also describe activities
> happening in the near future.
> I**'m playing** tennis this afternoon.
> We**'re having** pizza for dinner tonight.

4 Make more conversations with a partner.

1 these football boots? / John's / playing football later
2 these ballet shoes? / Mary's / going dancing tonight
3 this suitcase? / mine / going on holiday tomorrow
4 this coat? / Jane's / going for a walk soon
5 this plane ticket? / Jo's / flying to Rome this afternoon
6 all these glasses? / ours / having a party tonight

Check it

5 Correct the sentences.

1 Alice is tall and she's got long, black hairs.
2 Who's boots are these?
3 I'm wearing a jeans.
4 Look at Roger. He stands next to Jeremy.
5 He's work in a bank. He's the manager.
6 What is drinking Suzie?
7 Whose that man in the garden?
8 Where you going tonight?
9 What you do after school today?

GRAMMAR SPOT

1 Complete the table.

Subject	Object	Adjective	Pronoun
I	me	my	mine
You	you	_____	_____
He	_____	his	_____
She	_____	_____	hers
We	us	our	_____
They	them	_____	_____

2 *Whose . . . ?* asks about possession.

Whose hat is this?
Whose is this hat?   It's mine. = It's my hat.
Whose is it?

3 Careful!

Who's your teacher?   Who's = Who is

▶▶ **Grammar Reference 11.3 p132**

LISTENING AND SPEAKING
What a wonderful world!

1 Look out of the window. What can you see? Buildings? Hills? Fields? Can you see any people? What are they doing? Describe the scene.

2 These words often go together. Match them. Can you see any of them in the photos?

shake	clouds
babies	roses
sunny	hands
starry	trees
blue	day
red	night
white	cry
green	bloom
flowers	of the rainbow
colours	skies

3 Read the song by Louis Armstrong. Can you complete any of the lines? Many of the words are from exercise 2.

4 **T 11.5** Listen and complete the song.

What do you think?

Make a list of things that you think are wonderful in the world. Compare your list with a partner.

What a Wonderful World

I see _____ of green
red _____ too
I see them _____ for me and you
and I think to myself
what a wonderful world.
I see _____ of blue
and _____ of white
the bright _____ day
and the dark _____ night
and I think to myself
what a wonderful world.
The _____ of the rainbow
so pretty in the sky
are also on the _____
of the people going by.
I see friends shaking _____
saying, 'How do you do?'
They're really saying
'I _____ you.'
I hear _____ cry
I watch them grow.
They'll _____ much more
than you'll ever know
and I think to myself
what a wonderful world.
Yes, I think to myself
what a wonderful world.

VOCABULARY AND PRONUNCIATION
Words that rhyme

1 Match the words that rhyme.

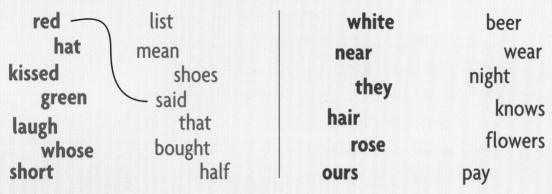

red	list	**white**	beer	
hat	mean	**near**	wear	
kissed	shoes	**they**	night	
green	said	**hair**	knows	
laugh	that	**rose**	flowers	
whose	bought	**ours**	pay	
short	half			

2 Write two of the words on each line according to the sound.

Vowels

1 /e/   <u>red</u>   <u>said</u>   5 /ɑː/ _____ _____

2 /æ/ _____ _____   6 /uː/ _____ _____

3 /ɪ/ _____ _____   7 /ɔː/ _____ _____

4 /iː/ _____ _____

Diphthongs

1 /aɪ/   <u>white</u>   _____   4 /eə/ _____ _____

2 /ɪə/ _____ _____   5 /əʊ/ _____ _____

3 /eɪ/ _____ _____   6 /aʊ/ _____ _____

T 11.6 Listen and check.

3 Can you add any more words to the lists? Practise saying the words in rhyming pairs.

Tongue twisters

4 **T 11.7** Tongue twisters are sentences that are difficult to say. They are good pronunciation practice. Listen, then try saying these quickly to a partner.

1 Four fine fresh fish for you

2 Six silly sisters selling shiny shoes

3 If a dog chews shoes, whose shoes does he choose?

4 I'm looking back,
To see if she's looking back,
To see if I'm looking back,
To see if she's looking back at me!

5 Choose two tongue twisters and learn them. Say them to the class.

EVERYDAY ENGLISH

In a clothes shop

1 Read the lines of conversation in a clothes shop. Who says them, the customer or the shop assistant?
Write **C** or **SA**.

a ☐ Can I help you? **SA**

b ☐ Oh yes. I like that one much better. Can I try it on? **C**

c ☐ £39.99. How do you want to pay?

d ☐ Yes, please. I'm looking for a shirt to go with my new suit.

e ☐ Blue.

f ☐ Yes, of course. The changing rooms are over there.

g ☐ OK. I'll take the white. How much is it?

h ☐ Can I pay by credit card?

i ☐ What colour are you looking for?

j ☐ No, it isn't the right blue.

k ☐ No, it's a bit too big. Have you got a smaller size?

l ☐ That's the last blue one we've got, I'm afraid. But we've got it in white.

m ☐ Well, what about this one? It's a bit darker blue.

n ☐ What about this one? Do you like this?

o ☐ Is the size OK?

p ☐ Credit card's fine. Thank you very much.

2 Can you match any lines?

Can I help you?

Yes, please. I'm looking for a shirt to go with my new suit.

What about this one? Do you like this?

No, it's not the right blue.

3 Work with a partner and put all the lines in the correct order.

T 11.8 Listen and check.

4 Practise the conversation with your partner. Make more conversations in a clothes shop. Buy some different clothes.

12 Life's an adventure!

going to future · Infinitive of purpose · The weather · Making suggestions

1 How many sentences can you make?

	soon.
I'm going to Florida	when I was a student.
I went to Florida	next month.
	in a year's time.
	two years ago.
	when I retire.

2 Make similar true sentences about you. Tell the class.

FUTURE PLANS
going to

1 Rosie and her teacher Miss Bishop both have plans for the future.
Read their future plans. Which do you think are Rosie's? Which are Miss Bishop's? Write **R** or **MB**.

1 [R] I'm going to be a ballet dancer.
2 ☐ I'm going to travel all over the world.
3 ☐ I'm going to learn Russian.
4 ☐ I'm going to learn to drive.
5 ☐ I'm going to open a school.
6 ☐ I'm not going to marry until I'm thirty-five.
7 ☐ I'm not going to wear skirts and blouses.
8 ☐ I'm going to wear jeans and T-shirts all the time.
9 ☐ I'm going to write a book.
10 ☐ I'm going to become a TV star.

T 12.1 Listen and check. Were you correct?

2 Talk first about Rosie, then about Miss Bishop. Use the ideas in exercise 1.

> *Rosie's going to be a ballet dancer.*

> *She's going to …*   > *She isn't going to …*

Which two plans are the same for both of them?

> *They're both going to …*

When I grow up …

Rosie, aged 11

3 **T 12.2** Listen and repeat the questions and answers about Rosie.

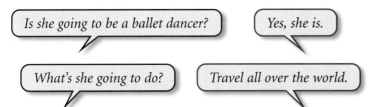

Is she going to be a ballet dancer?

Yes, she is.

What's she going to do?

Travel all over the world.

GRAMMAR SPOT

1 The verb *to be* + *going to* expresses future plans. Complete the table.

I	____	
You	____	
He/She	____	going to leave tomorrow.
We	____	
They	____	

What are the questions and the negatives?

2 Is there much difference between these two sentences?
  I'm leaving tomorrow.   I'm going to leave tomorrow.

▶▶ Grammar Reference 12.1 p133

When I retire ...

Miss Bishop, aged 59

PRACTICE

Questions about Rosie

1 With a partner, make more questions about Rosie. Then match them with an answer.

Questions
1 Why/she/learn French and Russian?
2 When/marry?
3 How many children/have?
4 How long/work?
5 What/teach?

Answers
a Until she's seventy-five.
b Two.
c Dancing.
d Not until she's thirty-five.
e Because she wants to dance in Paris and Moscow.

2 **T 12.3** Listen and check. Practise the questions and answers with your partner.

Questions about you

3 Are you going to do any of these things after the lesson? Ask and answer the questions with a partner.

1 watch TV

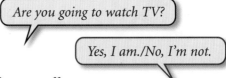

Are you going to watch TV?

Yes, I am./No, I'm not.

2 have a coffee
3 catch a bus
4 eat in a restaurant
5 meet some friends
6 cook a meal
7 go shopping
8 wash your hair
9 do your homework

4 Tell the class some of the things you and your partner *are* or are *not* going to do.

We're both going to have coffee.

I'm going to catch a bus, but Anna isn't. She's going to walk home.

I'm going to sneeze!

> ❗ We also use *going to* when we can see *now* that something is sure to happen in the future.

5 What is going to happen? Use these verbs.

> have   sneeze   win   jump   be late   kiss   rain   fall

1 It _____

2 You _____

3 I _____

4 They _____

5 She _____

6 He _____

7 He _____

8 They _____

6 Put a sentence from exercise 5 into each gap.

1 Take an umbrella. _____ .

2 Look at the time! _____ for the meeting.

3 Anna's running very fast. _____ .

4 Look! Jack's on the wall! _____ .

5 Look at that man! _____ .

6 _____ . It's due next month.

7 There's my sister and her boyfriend! Yuk! _____ .

8 'Oh dear. _____ . Aaattishooo!' 'Bless you!'

T 12.4 Listen and check.

92   Unit 12 · Life's an adventure!

I WANT TO TRAVEL THE WORLD
Infinitive of purpose

1 Match a country or a city with an activity. What can you see in the photographs?

Holland	visit the pyramids
Spain	fly over the Grand Canyon
Moscow	see Mount Fuji
Egypt	see the tulips
Kenya	walk along the Great Wall
India	watch flamenco dancing
China	take photographs of the lions
Japan	sunbathe on Copacabana beach
the USA	walk in Red Square
Rio	visit the Taj Mahal

2 Miss Bishop is going to visit all these countries. She is telling her friend, Harold, about her plans. Read their conversation and complete the last sentence.

Miss Bishop First I'm going to Holland.
Harold Why?
Miss Bishop To see the tulips, of course!
Harold Oh yes! How wonderful! Where are you going after that?
Miss Bishop Well, then I'm going to Spain to …

T 12.5 Listen and check. Practise the conversation with a partner.

GRAMMAR SPOT

1 With the verbs *to go* and *to come*, we usually use the Present Continuous for future plans.
   I'm going to Holland tomorrow.
   ✗ I'm going to go to Holland tomorrow.
   She's coming this evening.
   ✗ She's going to come this evening.

2 Do these sentences mean the same?
   I'm going to Holland to see the tulips.
   I'm going to Holland because I want to see the tulips.
   The infinitive can tell us why something happens.
   I'm going to America to learn English.

▶▶ **Grammar Reference 12.2 p133**

8

PRACTICE

Roleplay

1 Work with a partner. **Student A** is Harold, **Student B** is Miss Bishop. Ask and answer questions about the places.

Harold Why are you going to Holland?
Miss Bishop To see the tulips, of course!
Harold How wonderful!

2 Talk about Miss Bishop's journey. Use *first, then, next, after that.*

> *First she's going to Holland to see the tulips. Then she's …*

Why and *When*?

3 Write down the names of some places you went to in the past. Ask and answer questions about the places with a partner.

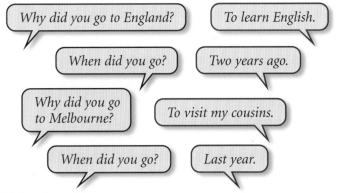

> *Why did you go to England?*   *To learn English.*
> *When did you go?*   *Two years ago.*
> *Why did you go to Melbourne?*   *To visit my cousins.*
> *When did you go?*   *Last year.*

Tell the class about your partner.

4 Write down the names of some places you are going to in the *future* and do the same.

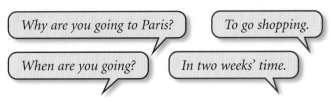

> *Why are you going to Paris?*   *To go shopping.*
> *When are you going?*   *In two weeks' time.*

Check it

5 Tick (✓) the correct sentence.
1 ☐ Is going to rain.
  ☐ It's going to rain.
2 ☐ Do you wash your hair this evening?
  ☐ Are you going to wash your hair this evening?
3 ☐ She's going to have a baby.
  ☐ She's going to has a baby.
4 ☐ I'm going to the Post Office to buy some stamps.
  ☐ I'm going to the Post Office for buy some stamps.
5 ☐ I'm going home early this evening.
  ☐ I'm go home early this evening.
6 ☐ I opened the window to get some fresh air.
  ☐ I opened the window for to get some fresh air.

READING AND SPEAKING
Living dangerously

1 Match a verb with a noun or phrase.

have	sick
win	an accident
feel	in water
float	top marks
get	a race

2 Which of these sports do you think is the most dangerous? Put them in order 1–6. 1 is the *most* dangerous. Compare your ideas with a partner and then the class.

- ☐ skiing
- ☐ football
- ☐ motor racing
- ☐ windsurfing
- ☐ golf
- ☐ sky-diving

3 Look at the photos of Clem Quinn and Sue Glass. Which of their sports would you most like to try? Why?

Work in two groups.

Group A Read about Clem.　**Group B** Read about Sue.

Answer the questions about your person. Check your answers with your group.

1 What happened when he/she was a child?
2 What job did he/she do when she/he grew up?
3 How did he/she become interested in the sport?
4 Why does he/she like the sport?
5 Does he/she think it is a dangerous sport?
6 Does he/she teach the sport?
7 What are his/her future plans?
8 When is he/she going to stop doing it?
9 These numbers are in your text. What do they refer to?
   5　6　20　100

4 Work with a partner from the other group. Compare Clem and Sue, using your answers.

Interviews

1 **Group A** You are Clem. Make questions about Sue.

1 Why/not like driving?
2 Why/Julian Swayland take you to Brands Hatch?
3 Why/do well on the motor racing course?
4 Why/stop motor racing?
5 What/do next year?

Group B You are Sue. Make questions about Clem.

1 What/do when you were five?
2 When/do your first parachute jump?
2 Why /move to the country?
3 Why/love sky-diving?
4 What/do next July?

2 Work with a partner from the other group. Interview each other.

Clem Quinn
SKY-DIVER

Clem Quinn was always interested in flying. When he was five, he tried to fly by jumping off the garden shed with a golf umbrella, but when he grew up he didn't become a pilot, he became a taxi driver. Then 20 years ago he did a parachute jump and loved it. He decided that being a taxi driver in London was a lot more dangerous than jumping out of a plane, so he moved to the country to learn parachute jumping and sky-diving. He is now a full-time teacher of sky-diving. He says:

'I love sky-diving because the world looks so good – blue sky, green fields, white clouds. You float through the air, it's like floating in water. You can see forever, all the way to the French coast. The views are fantastic. You can forget all your worries. People think it is dangerous but it's very safe. Football is much more dangerous. Footballers often have accidents. When did you last hear of a sky-diving accident? Next July I'm going to do a sky-dive with 100 people from six planes. That's a record. I'm never going to retire. I'm going to jump out of planes until I'm an old man.'

Sue Glass

RACING DRIVER

Sue Glass had a car accident when she was eight so she didn't like driving. When she grew up this was a problem, because she got a job with a car company. Then six years ago she met Julian Swayland, a racing driver, and she told him she was afraid of cars. He wanted to help, so he took her to Brands Hatch, a Grand Prix racing circuit. He drove her round corners at 100 mph and she loved it. Then she heard about a special motor racing course. She did the course with five men and was amazed when she got top marks. She says:

'I think I did well because I listened to everything the teacher said. I needed to because I was so afraid. The men often didn't listen. The best moment was my first championship race. I didn't win but I came fourth. I beat 20 men. I love the excitement of motor racing but it's a dangerous sport and I'm always very frightened. In fact I stopped doing it a year ago, because I got so nervous before each race, I felt really sick. I'm not going to race again, I'm going to teach other people to drive. I'm going to open a driving school next year.'

VOCABULARY AND SPEAKING
The weather

1 Match the words and symbols.

| sunny | rainy | windy | snowy | cloudy | foggy |

Which symbols can the following adjectives go with?

hot   warm   cold   cool   wet   dry

2 **T 12.6** Listen and complete the answers.

'What's the weather like today?' 'It's _____ and _____ .'

'What was it like yesterday?' 'Oh, it was _____ and _____ .'

'What's it going to be like tomorrow?' 'I think it's going to be _____ .'

 The question *What . . . like?* asks for a description.
What's the weather like? = Tell me about the weather.

Practise the questions and answers. Ask and answer about the weather where *you* are today, yesterday, and tomorrow.

3 Work with a partner. Find out about the weather round the world yesterday.

Student A Look at the information on this page.
Student B Look at the information from your teacher.

Ask and answer questions to complete the information.

> *What was the weather like in Athens?*

> *It was sunny and warm. 18 degrees.*

WORLD WEATHER: NOON YESTERDAY

		°C
Athens	S	18
Berlin	R	7
Bombay		
Edinburgh	C	5
Geneva		
Hong Kong	S	29
Lisbon		
London	R	10
Los Angeles		
Luxor	S	40
Milan		
Moscow	Sn	−1
Oslo		

S = sunny
C = cloudy
Fg = foggy
R = rainy
Sn = snowy

4 Which city was the hottest? Which was the coldest?
Which month do you think it is?

EVERYDAY ENGLISH

Making suggestions

1 Make a list of things you can do in good weather and things you can do in bad weather. Compare your list with a partner.

Good weather	Bad weather
go to the beach	watch TV

2 **T 12.7** Read and listen to the beginning of two conversations. Complete **B**'s suggestions.

1 **A** It's a lovely day!
    What shall we do?
 B Let's _____ !

2 **A** It's raining again!
    What shall we do?
 B Let's _____ and _____ .

> **!** 1 We use *shall* to ask for and make suggestions.
>   What shall we do?
>   Shall we go swimming? = I suggest that we go swimming.
> 2 We use *Let's* to make a suggestion for everyone.
>   Let's go! = I suggest that we all go. (Let's = Let us)
>   Let's have a pizza!

3 Match these lines with the two conversations in exercise 2. Put them in the correct order to complete the conversations.

Well, let's go to the beach.	Oh no! We watched a video last night.
OK. Which film do you want to see?	OK. I'll get my swimming costume.
Oh no! It's too hot to play tennis.	Well, let's go to the cinema.

T 12.8 Listen and check. Practise the conversations with your partner.

4 Have more conversations suggesting what to do when the weather is good or bad. Use your lists of activities in exercise 1 to help you.

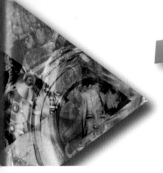

13 How terribly clever!

Question forms · Adverbs and adjectives · Describing feelings · Catching a train

STARTER

1 Match a question word with an answer.

2 Look at the answers. What do you think the story is?

When . . . ?	Six.
Where . . . ?	1991.
What . . . ?	Paris.
Who . . . ?	Because I love him.
Why . . . ?	John.
Which . . . ?	Some roses.
How . . . ?	£25.
How much . . . ?	The red ones.
How many . . . ?	By plane.

A QUIZ
Question words

1 Work in groups and answer the quiz.

2 **T 13.1** Listen and check your answers. Listen carefully to the intonation of the questions.

GRAMMAR SPOT

1 Underline all the question words in the quiz.

2 Make *two* questions for each of these statements, one with a question word and one without.

> I live in London. (where)
> *'Where do you live?' 'In London.'*
> *'Do you live in London?' 'Yes, I do.'*

1 She's wearing jeans. (what)
2 She works in the bank. (where)
3 He's leaving tomorrow. (when)
4 I visited my aunt. (who)
5 We came by taxi. (how)
6 They're going to have a party. (why)

3 What are the short answers to the questions?

▶▶ **Grammar Reference 13.1 p133**

3 In groups, write some general knowledge questions. Ask the class!

GENERAL KN

1 When did the first man walk on the moon?
   a 1961   b 1965   c 1969

2 Where are the Andes mountains?

3 Who did Mother Teresa look after?

4 Who won the last World Cup?

5 How many American states are there?

6 How much does an African elephant weigh?
   a 3–5 tonnes   b 5–7 tonnes   c 7–9 tonnes

7 How far is it from London to New York?

   a 6,000 kilometres

   b 9,000 kilometres

   c 12,000 kilometres

PRACTICE

Questions and answers

1 Look at the question words in **A** and the answers in **C**. Choose the correct question from **B**.

A	B	C
Where What When Who Why Which one How How much How many	did you buy? did you go? did you go with? did you pay?	To the shops. A new jacket. This morning. A friend from work. To buy some new clothes. The black, leather one. We drove. £120.99. Only one.

OWLEDGE QUIZ

8 How old was Princess Diana when she died?
a 33 **b** 36 **c** 39

9 What languages do Swiss people speak?

10 What did Marconi invent in 1901?

11 What sort of music did Louis Armstrong play?
a Jazz **b** Blues **c** Rock 'n' roll

12 What happens at the end of *Romeo and Juliet*?

13 What happened in Europe in 1939?

14 Why do birds migrate?

15 Which was the first country to have TV?
a Britain **b** the USA **c** Russia

16 Which language has the most words?
a French **b** Chinese **c** English

Listening and pronunciation

2 **T 13.2** Tick (✓) the sentence you hear.

1 ☐ Where do you want to go?
☐ Why do you want to go?

2 ☐ How is she?
☐ Who is she?

3 ☐ Where's he staying?
☐ Where's she staying?

4 ☐ Why did they come?
☐ Why didn't they come?

5 ☐ How old was she?
☐ How old is she?

6 ☐ Does he play the guitar?
☐ Did he play the guitar?

7 ☐ Where did you go at the weekend?
☐ Where do you go at the weekend?

Asking about you

3 Put the words in the correct order to make questions.

1 like learning do English you?

_____

2 do you night what did last?

_____

3 languages mother many does how your speak?

_____

4 last go you shopping did when?

_____

5 football which you do team support?

_____

6 come car today school by you to did?

_____

7 much do weigh you how?

_____

8 usually who sit you do next class in to?

_____

9 English want learn to you do why?

_____

4 Work with a partner. Ask and answer the questions.

DO IT CAREFULLY!
Adverbs and adjectives

1 Are the words in *italics* adjectives or adverbs?

1 Smoking is a *bad* habit.
The team played *badly* and lost the match.
2 Please listen *carefully*.
Jane's a *careful* driver.
3 The homework was *easy*.
Peter's very good at tennis. He won the game *easily*.
4 I know the Prime Minister *well*.
My husband's a *good* cook.
5 It's a *hard* life.
Teachers work *hard* and don't earn much money.

GRAMMAR SPOT

1 Look at these sentences.
Lunch is a quick meal for many people.
(*quick* = adjective. It describes a noun.)
I ate my lunch quickly.
(*quickly* = adverb. It describes a verb.)

2 How do we make regular adverbs? What happens when the adjective ends in -*y*?

3 There are two irregular adverbs in exercise 1. Find them.

▶▶ **Grammar Reference 13.2 p133**

---

2 Match the verbs or phrases with an adverb. Usually more than one answer is possible. Which are the irregular adverbs?

get up	slowly
walk	quietly
work	early
run	fluently
speak	carefully
speak English	easily
pass the exam	hard
do your homework	fast/quickly

PRACTICE

Order of adjectives/adverbs

1 Put the adjective in brackets in the correct place in the sentence. Where necessary, change the adjective to an adverb.

1 We had a holiday in Spain, but unfortunately we had weather. (terrible)
2 Maria dances. (good)
3 When I saw the accident, I phoned the police. (immediate)
4 Don't worry. Justin is a driver. (careful)
5 Jean-Pierre is a Frenchman. He loves food, wine, and rugby. (typical)
6 Please speak. I can't understand you. (slow)
7 We had a test today. (easy)
8 We all passed. (easy)
9 You speak English. (good)

Telling a story

2 Complete these sentences in a suitable way.

1 It started to rain. **Fortunately** …
2 Peter invited me to his party. **Unfortunately** …
3 I was fast asleep when **suddenly** …
4 I saw a man with a gun outside the bank. **Immediately** …

3 **T 13.3** Look at the picture and listen to a man describing what happened to him in the middle of the night. Number the adverbs in the order you hear them.

☐ quickly
☐ quietly
☐ slowly
☐ immediately
☐ carefully
☐ suddenly
☐ fortunately
☐ really

4 Work with a partner and tell the story again. Use the order of the adverbs to help you.

Check it

5 Each sentence has a mistake. Find it and correct it.

1 Where does live Anna's sister?
2 The children came into the classroom noisyly.
3 What means *whistle*?
4 I always work hardly.
5 Do you can help me, please?
6 When is going Peter on holiday?

VOCABULARY
Describing feelings

1 Match the feelings to the pictures.

| bored   tired   worried   excited   annoyed   interested |

2 Match the feelings and reasons to make sentences.

	Feelings		Reasons
I am	bored tired worried excited annoyed interested	because	I'm going on holiday tomorrow. we have a good teacher. I worked very hard today. I can't find my keys. I have nothing to do. I want to go to the party but I can't.

> ❗ Some adjectives can end in both *-ed* and *-ing*.
> The book was <u>interesting</u>.
> I was <u>interested</u> in the book.
> The lesson was <u>boring</u>.
> The students were <u>bored</u>.

3 Complete each sentence with the correct adjective.

1 **excited, exciting**
Life in New York is very …
The football fans were very …

2 **tired, tiring**
The marathon runners were very …
That game of tennis was very …

3 **annoyed, annoying**
The child's behaviour was really …
The teacher was … when nobody did the homework.

4 **worried, worrying**
The news is very …
Everybody was very … when they heard the news.

4 Answer your teacher's questions using adjectives from exercises 1 and 2.

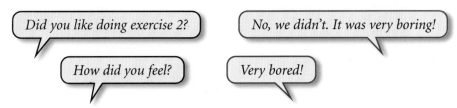

READING AND LISTENING
A story in a story

1 Think about when you were a small child. Did your parents tell you stories? Which was your favourite story? Tell the class.

2 Look at the first picture. Who do you think the people on the train are? Do they know each other?

3 **T 13.4** Read and listen to part one of the story.

4 Answer the questions.

1 Who are the people on the train?
2 What does Cyril ask questions about?
3 Why does the aunt tell the children a story?
4 What is the story about?
5 Do the children like the story?
6 Why does the young man start speaking?
7 Which of these adjectives best describe the people? Write them in the correct column.

quiet noisy badly-behaved tired worried bored boring annoyed annoying

The aunt

The children

The young man

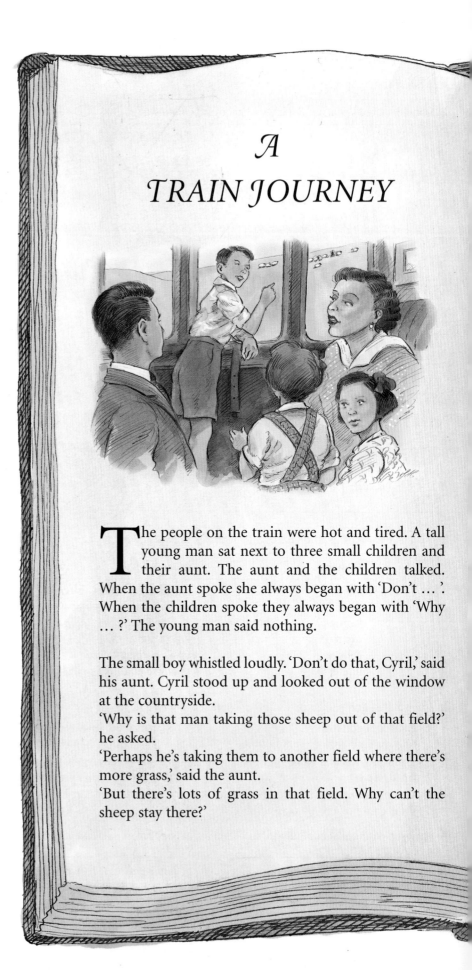

A
TRAIN JOURNEY

The people on the train were hot and tired. A tall young man sat next to three small children and their aunt. The aunt and the children talked. When the aunt spoke she always began with 'Don't … '. When the children spoke they always began with 'Why … ?' The young man said nothing.

The small boy whistled loudly. 'Don't do that, Cyril,' said his aunt. Cyril stood up and looked out of the window at the countryside.
'Why is that man taking those sheep out of that field?' he asked.
'Perhaps he's taking them to another field where there's more grass,' said the aunt.
'But there's lots of grass in that field. Why can't the sheep stay there?'

73

'Perhaps the grass in the other field is better.'
'Why is it better?'
The young man looked annoyed.
'Oh dear,' thought the aunt, 'he doesn't like children.'
'Sit down quietly, Cyril. Now, listen, I'm going to tell you all a story.'

The children looked bored but they listened. The story was very boring indeed. It was about a very beautiful little girl, who worked hard and behaved beautifully. Everybody loved her. One day she fell into a lake and everyone in the village ran to save her.

'Why did they save her?' asked the bigger girl.
'Because she was so good,' said the aunt.
'But that's stupid,' said the girl. 'When people fall into lakes, it doesn't matter if they're good or bad, you run to save them.'
'You're right,' said the young man, speaking for the first time. 'That's a ridiculous story.'
'Well, perhaps *you* would like to tell a story,' said the aunt coldly.
'OK,' said the man. The children looked interested and he began.

5 The young man tells the story of a little girl called Bertha. Look at the pictures. What do you think happened to Bertha?

6 Read and listen to part two.

74

The tale of horribly good Bertha

'Once upon a time, a long time ago there was a little girl called Bertha. She was always well behaved and worked hard at school to please her parents and her teachers. She was never late, never dirty or untidy, never rude, and she never told lies.'

The children on the train began to look bored. 'Was she pretty?' asked the smaller girl.
'No,' said the young man. 'She wasn't pretty at all. She was just *horribly* good. Bertha was so good that she won three gold medals. One said *Never late*, one said *Always polite*, and the third said *Best Child in the World*.'

'Yuk!' said the three children.

'Anyway,' said the young man, 'Bertha was so good that the king invited her to his palace. So she put on her best clean white dress and she pinned her three medals to the

75

front and she walked through the woods to the king's palace. But in the woods there lived a big hungry wolf. He saw Bertha's lovely white dress through the trees and he heard the medals clinking together as she walked.

'Aha!' thought the wolf. 'Lunch!' And he started to move quickly but quietly through the trees towards Bertha.'

'Oh, no!' cried the children. 'Is he going to eat Bertha?'

'Yes, of course,' answered the young man. 'Bertha tried to run away but she couldn't run fast because the medals were so heavy. The wolf caught her easily and he ate everything, every bit of Bertha, except her three medals.'

'That's a terrible story,' said the aunt.
'No it isn't,' shouted the children. 'It's the best story ever!'
'Ah,' said the young man, 'the train's stopping. It's my station.'

7 Answer the questions.
1 What is the same and what is different in the aunt's story and the young man's story?
2 Does the aunt like the young man's story? Why/Why not?
3 Do the children like the story? Why/Why not?
4 Which of these do you think is the moral of Bertha's story?

> It pays to be good.
> It never pays to be good.
> It doesn't always pay to be good.

8 Tell the story of Bertha. Use the pictures in exercise 5 on p103 to help you.

Language work

1 Put some adjectives and adverbs from the story of Bertha into the correct box.

Adjectives	Adverbs

2 Write questions about Bertha's story using these question words. Ask and answer the questions across the class.

> ~~when~~ how many what why where how

> *When did the story take place?*   *A long time ago.*

EVERYDAY ENGLISH
Catching a train

1 Ann is phoning to find out the times of trains to Bristol.

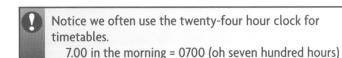 Listen and write in the arrival times.

> ❗ Notice we often use the twenty-four hour clock for timetables.
> 7.00 in the morning = 0700 (oh seven hundred hours)

DEPARTURE TIME from OXFORD	ARRIVAL TIME at Bristol Temple Meads
0816	
0945	
1040	

2 **T 13.7** Ann is at Oxford Station. Listen and complete the conversation. Then practise with a partner.

A Good morning. (1) _____ the times of trains (2) _____ Bristol (3) _____ Oxford, please?

B Afternoon, evening? When (4) _____ ?

A About five o'clock this afternoon.

B About (5) _____ . Right. Let's have a look. There's a train that (6) _____ 5.28, then there isn't (7) _____ until 6.50.

A And (8) _____ get in?

B The 5.28 gets into Oxford at 6.54 and the 6.50 (9) _____ .

A Thanks a lot.

3 Ann goes to the ticket office. Put the lines of the conversation in the correct order.

☐ **A** Hello. A return to Bristol, please. [1]

☐ **A** A day return.

☐ **C** How do you want to pay?

☐ **A** OK, thanks very much. Goodbye. [11]

☐ **C** Here's your change and your ticket.

☐ **C** You want platform 1 over there.

☐ **A** Here's a twenty-pound note.

☐ **C** Day return or period return?

☐ **A** Cash, please.

☐ **C** That's eighteen pounds.

☐ **A** Thank you. Which platform is it?

T 13.8 Listen and check. Practise the conversation with a partner.

4 Make more conversations with your partner. Look at the information from your teacher. Decide where you want to go. Find out about times, then buy your ticket.

14 Have you ever?

Present Perfect + *ever*, *never*, *yet*, and *just* · At the airport

1 Match the countries and flags.

| Australia | Brazil | France | Germany | Great Britain |
| Greece | Hungary | Italy | Japan | Canada | Spain | the USA |

1 _____ 2 _____ 3 _____ 4 _____ 5 _____ 6 _____

7 _____ 8 _____ 9 _____ 10 _____ 11 _____ 12 _____

2 Tick (✓) the countries that you have visited.

IN MY LIFE
Present Perfect + *ever* and *never*

1 **T 14.1** Read and listen to the sentences. Then listen and repeat.

I've been to Germany. (I've = I have)
I haven't been to France.
I've been to the USA.
I've never been to Australia.
I haven't been to any of the countries!

Work in groups. Tell each other which of the countries above you have or haven't been to. Have you been to any other countries?

2 **T 14.2** Read and listen to the conversation. Practise with a partner.

A Have you ever been to Paris?
B No, I haven't.
A Have you ever been to Berlin?
B Yes, I have.
A When did you go?
B Two years ago.

EL CAPITAN — SUNSET
YOSEMITE NATIONAL PARK, CALIFORNIA
Rising over 3,245 feet above the valley floor, El Capitan is one of the largest exposed monoliths in the world.
© Photograph by Chris Loberg

Hi guys!
San Francisco is fantastic! We are having a superb time - and are trying to see all the sights. We're staying near the Yosemite National Park, which is just beautiful.
See you guys soon (probably read this with you actually)
Nicky

thought about ....
The weather is fantastic. We went to an Aussie football match yesterday and are off to a winery & then a 'barbie' tomorrow.

3 Write down the names of four cities in your country or another country that you have been to. Have similar conversations with your partner.

4 Tell the class about your partner.

> *Maria's been to Berlin.* (Maria's = Maria has)

> *She went there two years ago.*

> *But she hasn't been to Paris. / She's never been to Paris.* (She's = She has)

BUDAPEST

GRAMMAR SPOT

1 We use the Present Perfect to talk about experiences in our lives.
   Have you ever (at any time in your life) been to Paris?

2 We use the Past Simple to say exactly *when* something happened.
   When did you go to Paris?

I went there	last year.
	two years ago.
	in 1998.

3 We make the Present Perfect tense with *has/have* + the past participle.
   Complete the table.

	Positive	Negative	
I/You/We/They	_____	_____	been to Paris.
He/She/It	_____	_____	

4 Write *ever* and *never* in the right place in these sentences.
   Has he _____ been to London?
   He's _____ been to London.

▶▶ **Grammar Reference 14.1 p134**

Cidade Antiga
LISBOA

PRACTICE

Past participles

1 Here are the past participles of some verbs. Write the infinitive.

eaten __eat__	made _____	given _____
seen _____	taken _____	won _____
met _____	driven _____	had _____
drunk _____	cooked _____	stayed _____
flown _____	bought _____	done _____

2 Which are the two regular verbs?

3 What are the Past Simple forms of the verbs?

4 Look at the list of irregular verbs on p142 and check your answers.

PARIS

The life of Ryan

1 **T 14.3** Listen to Ryan talking about his life and tick (✓) the things he has done.

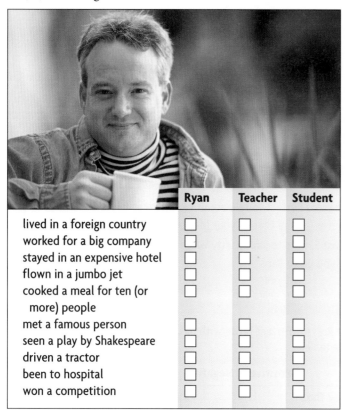

	Ryan	Teacher	Student
lived in a foreign country	☐	☐	☐
worked for a big company	☐	☐	☐
stayed in an expensive hotel	☐	☐	☐
flown in a jumbo jet	☐	☐	☐
cooked a meal for ten (or more) people	☐	☐	☐
met a famous person	☐	☐	☐
seen a play by Shakespeare	☐	☐	☐
driven a tractor	☐	☐	☐
been to hospital	☐	☐	☐
won a competition	☐	☐	☐

2 Tell your teacher about Ryan and answer your teacher's questions.

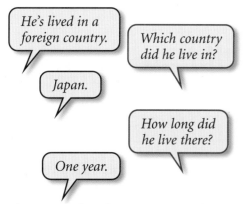

He's lived in a foreign country.

Which country did he live in?

Japan.

How long did he live there?

One year.

3 Ask your teacher the questions and complete the chart.

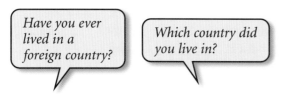

Have you ever lived in a foreign country?

Which country did you live in?

4 Ask a partner the questions. Tell the class about your partner.

A HONEYMOON IN LONDON
Present Perfect + *yet* and *just*

1 Rod and Marilyn come from Christchurch, New Zealand. They are on honeymoon in London. Before they went, they made a list of things they wanted to do there. Read the list below.

2 **T 14.4** Marilyn is phoning her sister Judy, back home in New Zealand. Listen to their conversation. Tick (✓) the things she and Rod have done.

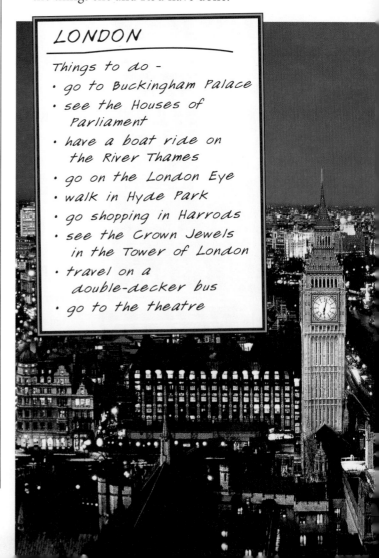

LONDON

Things to do –
• go to Buckingham Palace
• see the Houses of Parliament
• have a boat ride on the River Thames
• go on the London Eye
• walk in Hyde Park
• go shopping in Harrods
• see the Crown Jewels in the Tower of London
• travel on a double-decker bus
• go to the theatre

GRAMMAR SPOT

1 Complete the sentences.
  1 Have you _____ the Crown Jewels **yet**?
  2 We _____ been to the theatre **yet**.
  3 We've **just** _____ a boat ride on the Thames.

2 Where do we put *yet* in a sentence? Where do we put *just* in a sentence?

3 We can only use *yet* with **two** of the following. Which two?
  ☐ Positive sentences
  ☐ Questions
  ☐ Negative sentences

▶▶ **Grammar Reference 14.2 p134**

3 Look at the list with a partner. Say what Rod and Marilyn have done and what they haven't done yet.

> *They've travelled on a double-decker bus.*

> *They haven't seen the Crown Jewels yet.*

T 14.4 Listen again and check.

PRACTICE

I've just done it

1 Work with a partner. Make questions with *yet* and answers with *just*.

> *Have you done the washing-up yet?*

> *Yes, I've just done it.*

  1 do the washing-up
  2 do the shopping
  3 wash your hair
  4 clean the car
  5 make the dinner
  6 meet the new student
  7 have a coffee
  8 give your homework to the teacher
  9 finish the exercise

Check it

2 Tick (✓) the correct sentence.
  1 ☐ I saw John yesterday.
    ☐ I've seen John yesterday.
  2 ☐ Did you ever eat Chinese food?
    ☐ Have you ever eaten Chinese food?
  3 ☐ Donna won £5,000 last month.
    ☐ Donna has won £5,000 last month.
  4 ☐ I've never drank champagne.
    ☐ I've never drunk champagne.
  5 ☐ Tom has ever been to America.
    ☐ Tom has never been to America.
  6 ☐ Has your sister yet had the baby?
    ☐ Has your sister had the baby yet?
  7 ☐ I haven't finished my homework yet.
    ☐ I've finished my homework yet.
  8 ☐ Did she just bought a new car?
    ☐ Has she just bought a new car?

READING AND SPEAKING
How to live to be 100

1 Who is the oldest person you know? How old is he/she? What do you know about their lives? Why do you think they have lived so long? Tell the class.

2 These words are in the texts. Write them in the correct column.

pneumonia   ambulance driver   engineer   heart attack
lung cancer   rheumatic fever   secretary   dressmaker

Jobs	Illnesses

3 Read the introduction. Are similar facts true for your country?

How to live to be 100

More and more people are living to be 100 years old. There are now 4,400 centenarians in Britain – 10 times more than there were 40 years ago. Professor Grimley Evans of Oxford University believes that future generations will live even longer, to 115 years and more. Here are the stories of three people who have lived to be 100.

4 Work in groups of three. Each choose a different person and read about her/him. Answer the questions.

1 What jobs has she/he had in her/his life?
2 Where does he/she live now?
3 Which countries has she/he been to?
4 Did he/she marry and have children?
5 Is her husband/his wife still alive?
6 When and why did she/he give up smoking cigarettes?
7 What do you learn about other people in his/her family?
8 Has she/he ever been very ill?
9 What food does he/she like?
10 What exercise does she/he like doing?

5 Work with your group. Compare the three people, using your answers.

What do you think?

- Why do you think these people have lived so long? How many reasons can you find?
- Would you like to live to be 100? Why/why not?

Joyce Bews

Joyce Bews was 100 last year. She was born and grew up in Portsmouth on the south coast of England, where she still lives. For many years she was a dressmaker, and she didn't marry until she was 65. Her husband died of lung cancer only 10 weeks after they married. It was then that she gave up smoking. Joyce has had only one serious illness in her life – she had pneumonia when she was 20. She has lived in Australia and America. She lived in Australia after her husband died, and she went to America when she was 75. She has just returned from a holiday in Spain with her niece, aged 75. She says: 'I'm not sure why I've lived so long. I've never exercised but I've always eaten well, lots of fruit. My youngest brother has just died, aged 90.'

Alice Patterson-Smythe

Alice Patterson-Smythe was born just over 100 years ago in Edinburgh. She now lives in Norfolk. She drove ambulances in the First World War, and worked as a school secretary until she retired. She has been a widow for 25 years and has three children, six grandchildren, and 11 great-grandchildren. She smoked quite a lot when she was a young girl but she gave up when she was 68 because she had a heart attack. Her nineties were the best years of her life because her millionaire grandson took her on his aeroplane to visit Tokyo, Los Angeles, and Miami. She says: 'I love life. I play golf once a week and do Latin American dancing, and I eat lots of fruit and vegetables. We are a long-lived family – my mother was 95 when she died.'

Tommy Harrison

Tommy Harrison is exactly 100 years old. He's a retired engineer. His wife, Maude, died 14 years ago. They had no children and now he lives alone in his flat in Bristol. Tommy has smoked all his life. First he smoked cigarettes, about 10 a day, but 40 years ago he changed to a pipe. He has only been ill once in his life, and that was just before the First World War, when he had rheumatic fever. The only time he visits his doctor is to get a certificate to say that he can still drive his car. Every day he has a full English breakfast – bacon, eggs, toast and marmalade. He has only been abroad once, to France during the war. He says: 'I still go dancing and swimming but I don't want to live for ever, perhaps 12 more months. My father lived until he was 99.'

LISTENING
Leaving on a jet plane

1 **T 14.5** Close your books and your eyes and listen to a song. What is it about?

2 Read the words of the song. Choose the word on the right which best completes the line.

Leaving on a jet plane

All my (1)_____ are packed, I'm ready to go,	1 bags suitcases
I'm standing here outside your (2)_____ ,	2 window door
I (3)_____ to wake you up to say goodbye,	3 hate want
But the dawn is breaking,	
It's early morn',	
The taxi's (4)_____ ,	4 here waiting
He's blowing his (5)_____ ,	5 horn trumpet
Already I'm so lonesome	
I could (6)_____ .	6 cry die
Chorus So kiss me and (7)_____ for me,	7 laugh smile
(8)_____ me that you'll wait for me,	8 tell say
(9)_____ me like you'll never let me go,	9 love hold
'Cos I'm leaving on a jet plane,	
I don't know when I'll be back again.	
Oh babe, I hate to go.	
There's so (10)_____ times I've let you down,	10 much many
So many times I've (11)_____ around,	11 played walked
I tell you now	
They don't mean a thing.	
Every (12)_____ I go, I'll think of you	12 time place
Every song I sing, I'll sing for you	
When I (13)_____ back	13 come go
I'll wear your wedding (14)_____ .	14 ring dress

3 Listen again and check the words. Sing along!

EVERYDAY ENGLISH
At the airport

1 What do you do at an airport? Read the sentences and put them in the correct order.

- ☐ You wait in the departure lounge.
- ☐ You board the plane.
- ☐ You get a trolley for your luggage.
- ☐ *1* You arrive at the airport.
- ☐ You check in your luggage and get a boarding pass.
- ☐ You go through passport control.
- ☐ You check the departures board for your gate number.

2 **T 14.6** Listen to the airport announcements and complete the chart.

FLIGHT NUMBER	DESTINATION	GATE NUMBER	REMARK	
B A 5 1 6	G E N E V A	4	LAST CALL	
S K ☐	☐	☐	DELAYED	☐
A F ☐	☐	☐	NOW BOARDING GATE	☐
L H ☐	☐	☐	NOW BOARDING GATE	☐
V S ☐	☐	☐	WAIT IN LOUNGE	

3 **T 14.7** Listen to the conversations. Who are the people? Where are they? Choose from these places.

- in the arrival hall
- in the departure lounge
- at the departure gate
- at the check-in desk

4 Complete each conversation with the correct question.

> When can we see each other again?
> Did you have a good honeymoon?
> Did the announcement say gate 4 or 14?
> have you got much hand luggage?

1 **A** Listen! … BA 516 to Geneva. That's our flight.
  B _____ ?
  A I couldn't hear. I think it said 4.
  B Look! There it is on the departure board. It *is* gate 4.
  A OK. Come on! Let's go.

2 **A** Can I have your ticket, please?
  B Yes, of course.
  A Thank you. How many suitcases have you got?
  B Just one.
  A And _____ ?
  B Just this bag.
  A That's fine.
  B Oh … can I have a seat next to the window?
  A Yes, that's OK. Here's your boarding pass. Have a nice flight!

T 14.7 Listen and check. Practise the conversations with a partner.

5 Work with a partner. Make more conversations at each of the places.

3 **A** Rod! Marilyn! Over here!
  B Hi! Judy! Great to see you!
  A It's great to see you too. You look terrific!
  _____ ?
  B Fantastic. Everything was fantastic.
  A Well, you haven't missed anything here. Nothing much has happened at all!

4 **A** There's my flight. It's time to go.
  B Oh no! It's been a wonderful two weeks. I can't believe it's over.
  A I know. _____ ?
  B Soon, I hope. I'll write every day.
  A I'll phone too. Goodbye.
  B Goodbye. Give my love to your family.

Tapescripts

Unit 1

T 1.1   see p6

T 1.2

A   Hello. My name's Richard. What's your name?
B   Kurt.
A   Where are you from, Kurt?
B   I'm from Hamburg. Where are you from?
A   I'm from London.

T 1.3   see p7

T 1.4   Listen carefully!

1   He's from Spain.
2   What's her name?
3   They're from Brazil.
4   Where's she from?
5   He's a teacher in Italy.

T 1.5   see p9

T 1.6   Yasmina

My name's Yasmina Kamal and I'm a student. I'm 19. I'm not married. I have one sister and two brothers. I live in a flat in Cairo, Egypt. I want to learn English because it's an international language.

T 1.7   The alphabet song

A B C D E F G
H I J K L M N O P
L M N O P Q R S T
L M N O P Q R S T
U V W X Y Z

That is the English alphabet!

T 1.8   see p10

T 1.9   Telephone numbers

682 947
8944 5033
020 7399 7050

T 1.10   What are the numbers?

1   Hello. 01913 786 499.
2   My brother has four children.
3   I have 10 stamps in my bag.
4   Hello, extension 4177.
5   I live at number 19.
6   Goodbye. See you at five.

T 1.11   Everyday conversations

1   Hello, extension 3442.
    Hello, Mary. This is Edward. How are you?
    I'm fine, thank you. And you?
    I'm OK, thanks.

2   Goodbye, Marcus.
    Goodbye, Bianca. Have a nice day.
    Thanks, Marcus. See you this evening!
    Yes, at seven in the cinema.

3   Hello, 270899.
    Hi, Flora! It's me, Leo. How are you?
    Not bad, thanks. And you?
    Very well. How are the children?
    They're fine.

Unit 2

T 2.1   Keesha Anderson

1   A   What's her surname?
    B   Anderson.
2   A   What's her first name?
    B   Keesha.
3   A   Where's she from?
    B   London, England.
4   A   What's her job?
    B   She's a journalist.
5   A   What's her address?
    B   42, Muswell Hill Road, London N10 3JD.
6   A   What's her phone number?
    B   020 8863 5741.
7   A   How old is she?
    B   Twenty-eight.
8   A   Is she married?
    B   No, she isn't.

T 2.2   see p13

T 2.3   see p14

T 2.4   Adjectives

1   He's old. She's young.
2   It's easy. It's difficult.
3   It's new. It's old.
4   It's fast. It's slow.
5   It's lovely. It's horrible.
6   They're hot. They're cold.
7   They're cheap. They're expensive.
8   It's small. It's big.

T 2.5   see p17

T 2.6   Dorita in New York

D = Dorita   O = Orlando
1   D   Hello. My name's Dorita.
    O   Hello, Dorita. I'm Orlando.
    D   Where are you from, Orlando?
    O   I'm from Italy, from Rome. And you? Where are you from?
    D   I'm from Argentina.
    O   From Buenos Aires?
    D   Yes, that's right.

I = Isabel   C = class   D = Dorita
2   I   Good morning everybody.
    C   Good morning, Isabel.
    I   How are you all?
    C   Fine.
        Good.
        OK.
    I   How are you Dorita?
    D   I'm fine thank you. And you?
    I   Very well. Now listen everybody …

M = Marnie   D = Dorita   A = Annie
3   M   Bye, Dorita. Have a nice day.
    D   Pardon?
    A   Have a good day at the school of English.
    D   Oh, yes. Thank you. Same to you.
    M   What's your teacher called?
    D   My teacher called?
    A   Your teacher's name – what is it?
    D   Ah, yes. Her name's Isabel.
    M   And is she good?
    D   My teacher good?
    A   Yeah. Isabel, your teacher, is she a good teacher?
    D   Oh yes, yes. Very good, very nice.

T 2.7   see p18

T 2.8

1   That's five pounds fifty, please.
2   Look, it's only twelve pounds.
3   Here you are. Twenty p change.
4   Pizza is three pounds seventy-five.
5   One hundred pounds for that is very expensive.
6   Nine pounds fif*teen*, not nine pounds fifty.

T 2.9   see p19

T 2.10   In a snack bar

1   A   Good morning.
    B   Good morning. Can I have an orange juice, please?
    A   Here you are. Anything else?
    B   No, thanks.
    A   Ninety p, please.
    B   Thanks.
    A   Thank you.

2   A   Hi. Can I help?
    B   Yes. Can I have a tuna and egg salad, please?
    A   Anything to drink?
    B   Yeah. A mineral water, please.
    A   OK. Here you are.
    B   How much is that?
    A   Four pounds ninety-five, please.
    B   Thanks.

Unit 3

T 3.1 see p20

T 3.2
1 She's a scientist. He's a doctor.
2 Alison comes from England. Bob comes from England, too.
3 She lives in a big city, but he lives in a small town.
4 She works three days a week. He works 16 hours a day non-stop.
5 He speaks to sick people on his radio. She speaks three languages.
6 She loves her job and he loves his job, too.
7 She has a daughter. He isn't married.
8 She likes skiing and going for walks in her free time. He never has free time.

T 3.3 Questions and answers
Where does Alison come from? Cambridge, in England.
What does she do? She's a scientist.
Does she speak French? Yes, she does.
Does she speak Spanish? No, she doesn't.

T 3.4
1 Where does Bob come from? England.
2 What does he do? He's a doctor.
3 Does he fly to help people? Yes, he does.
4 Does he speak French and German? No, he doesn't.

T 3.5 Is it true or false?
1 Philippe comes from Paris.
2 Philippe lives in London.
3 He works in the centre of Paris.
4 He speaks English very well.
5 He's married.
6 Keiko lives and works in New York.
7 She speaks French and German.
8 She plays tennis in her free time.
9 She isn't married.
10 Mark works in an office in Moscow.
11 He has three sons.
12 He likes playing football in his free time.

T 3.6 Listen carefully!
1 She likes her job.
2 She loves walking.
3 He isn't married.
4 Does he have three children?
5 What does he do?

T 3.7 Mr McSporran's day
1 A Good afternoon. Can I have two ice-creams, please?
  B Chocolate or vanilla?
  A One chocolate, one vanilla please.
  B That's £1.80. Anything else?
  A No, thank you.

2 A Only two letters for you this morning, Mrs Craig.
  B Thank you very much, Mr McSporran. And how's Mrs McSporran this morning?
  A Oh, she's very well, thank you. She's busy in the shop.

3 A A glass of wine before bed, my dear?
  B Oh, yes please.
  A Here you are.
  B Thank you, my dear. I'm very tired this evening.

4 A Hello Mr McSporran!
  B Good morning, boys and girls. Hurry up, we're late.
  A Can I sit here, Mr McSporran?
  C No, no, I want to sit there.
  B Be quiet all of you, and SIT DOWN!

T 3.8 What time is it?
It's five o'clock.   It's eight o'clock.
It's half past five.   It's half past eleven.
It's quarter past five.   It's quarter past two.
It's quarter to six.   It's quarter to nine.
It's five past five.   It's ten past five.
It's twenty past five.   It's twenty-five past five.
It's twenty-five to six.   It's twenty to six.
It's ten to six.   It's five to six.

T 3.9 see p27

Unit 4

T 4.1 Bobbi Brown's weekdays
My weekends are fast and exciting. My weekdays are fast and domestic! I have two sons, Dylan 7, and Dakota 5. Every morning I get up one hour before them, at 6.00, and I go to the gym. I come home and I make breakfast, then I take them to school. On Mondays I always go shopping. I buy all the food for the week. I often cook dinner in the evenings, but not every day because I don't like cooking. Fortunately, my husband, Don, loves cooking. On Tuesdays and Thursdays I visit my father. He lives on the next block. Every afternoon I pick up the kids from school. In the evenings Don and I usually relax, but sometimes we visit friends. We never go out on Friday evenings because I start work so early on Saturdays.

T 4.2 Questions and answers
B = Bobbi
A Where do you work?
B In New York.
A Do you like your work?
B Yes, I do.
A Do you relax at weekends?
B No, I don't.
A Why don't you relax at weekends?
B Because I work.

T 4.3
1 What time do you go to bed?
  At 11 o'clock.
2 Where do you go on holiday?
  To Spain or Portugal.
3 What do you do on Sundays?
  I always relax.
4 When do you do your homework?
  After dinner.
5 Who do you live with?
  My mother and sisters.
6 Why do you like your job?
  Because it's interesting.
7 How do you travel to school?
  By bus.
8 Do you go out on Friday evenings?
  Yes, I do sometimes.

T 4.4 Listen carefully!
1 What does she do on Sundays?
2 Do you stay home on Thursday evenings?
3 He lives here.
4 What do you do on Saturday evenings?
5 I read a lot.
6 Why don't you like your job?

T 4.5 Favourite seasons
1 **Al Wheeler from Canada**
We have long, cold winters and short, hot summers. We have a holiday home near a lake, so in summer I go sailing a lot and I play baseball, but in winter I often play ice hockey and go ice-skating. My favourite season is autumn, or fall, as we say in North America. I love the colours of the trees – red, gold, orange, yellow, and brown.

2 **Manuela da Silva from Portugal**
People think it's always warm and sunny in Portugal, but January and February are often cold, wet, and grey. I don't like winter. I usually meet friends in restaurant and bars and we chat. Sometimes we go to a Brazilian bar. I love Brazilian music. But then suddenly it's summer and at weekends we drive to the beach, sunbathe, and go swimming. I love summer.

3 **Toshi Suzuki from Japan**
I work for Pentax cameras, in the export department. I don't have a lot of free time, but I have one special hobby – taking photographs, of course! I like taking photographs of flowers, especially in spring. Sometimes, after work, I relax in a bar near my office with friends. My friend, Shigeru, likes singing pop songs in the bar. This has a special name, *karaoke*. I don't sing – I'm too shy!

T 4.6 Who's who?

M = Manuela   J = Jane
F = Manuela's friends

1 **M** Hello, everybody! This is my friend Jane from England.
   F Hi!
      Hello!
      Hello Jane!
   J Hello. Pleased to meet you.
   M Sit down here, Jane.
   J Thanks.
   F Do you like the music, Jane?
   J Yes, I do. Is it American?
   F No, it's Brazilian jazz!
   M Come and have a drink, Jane.

T = Toshi   J = Ann Jones

2 **T** Mrs Jones! How do you do?
   J How do you do?
   T Please come in. You're from our office in London, aren't you?
   J Yes, that's right.
   T Welcome to Tokyo! Do you like our headquarters here?
   J Yes. It's very big. How many people work here?
   T About six thousand people. Do you want to see our offices?

A = Al   M = Mick

3 **A** What do you want to do today, Mick?
   M Ooh, I don't know. What do you …
   A Ah! Do you like sailing?
   M Yes, very much. I sometimes go sailing in Scotland but not very often.
   A OK – so today it's sailing and fishing on the lake.
   M Fantastic. I love fishing too – we go fishing a lot in Scotland.

T 4.7 Everyday conversations

1 **A** I'm sorry I'm late. The traffic is bad today.
   B Don't worry. Come and sit down. We're on page 25.

2 **A** Excuse me.
   B Yes?
   A Do you have a dictionary?
   B I'm sorry, I don't. It's at home.
   A That's OK.

3 **A** It's very hot in here. Can I open the window?
   B Really? I'm quite cold.
   A OK. It doesn't matter.

4 **A** Excuse me!
   B Can I help you?
   A Can I have a film for my camera?
   B How many exposures?
   A Pardon?
   B How many *exposures*?
   A What does 'exposures' mean
   B How many pictures? 24? 36? 40?
   A Ah! Now I understand! 40, please.

Unit 5

T 5.1 Questions and answers

A Is there a television?
B Yes, there is.
A Is there a radio?
B No, there isn't.
A Are there any books?
B Yes, there are.
A How many books are there?
B There are a lot.
A Are there any photographs?
B No, there aren't.

T 5.2 Description of a living room

There are three people in the living room. A man and a woman on the sofa and a little girl in the armchair. There's a radio on the coffee table and a rug under it. There's a cat on the rug in front of the fire. There are a lot of pictures on the walls but there aren't any photographs. There are two plants on the floor next to the television and some flowers on the small table next to the sofa.

T 5.3 Helen's kitchen

H = Helen   B = Bob

H And this is the kitchen.
B Mmm, it's very nice.
H Well, it's not very big, but there are a lot of cupboards. And there's a new fridge, and a cooker. That's new, too.
B But what's *in* all these cupboards?
H Well, not a lot. There are some cups, but there aren't any plates. And I have some knives and forks, but I don't have any spoons!
B Do you have any glasses?
H No. Sorry.
B Never mind. We can drink this champagne from those cups! Cheers!

T 5.4 What's in Pierre's briefcase?

What's in my briefcase? Well, there's a newspaper – a French newspaper – and there's a dictionary – my French/English dictionary. I have some pens, three I think. Also I have a notebook for vocabulary, I write words in that every day. And of course I have my keys, my car keys and my house keys. Oh yes, very important, there are some photos of my family, my wife and my daughter and there's my mobile phone. I ring my home in Paris every night. That's all I think. I don't have any stamps and my address book is in my hotel.

T 5.5 Homes around the world

1 Manola from Lisbon

I live in the old town near the sea. It is called the Alfama. I have a very beautiful flat. There's just *one* room in my flat, one very big room with one very big window. My bed's next to the window so I see the sea and all the lights of the city when I go to sleep. I live alone, but I have a cat and I'm near the shops and lots of friends come to visit me. I love my flat.

2 Ray and Elsie from Toronto

Elsie Our house is quite old, about fifty years old. It's quite near to the city centre. We have a living room, quite a big kitchen and three bedrooms, but the room we all love is our family room.
Ray Yes, there's a TV and a stereo and a large comfortable sofa in there, and some big, old armchairs. We love sitting there in winter with the snow outside.
Elsie Our children aren't at home now, they both have jobs in the USA, so most of the time it's just Ray and me.

3 Brad from Malibu

My house is fantastic. It's right next to the sea. My neighbours are very rich. Some of them are famous film stars. In my house there are ten rooms, five are bedrooms, and everything is white, the floors, the walls, the sofas, everything. I also have a swimming pool, a cinema and an exercise room. I live here alone. I'm not married at the moment. My ex-wife is French. She lives in Paris now with our three sons.

4 Alise from Samoa

I live with my family in a house near the sea. We have an open house, … er … that is … er … our house doesn't have any walls. Houses in Samoa don't have walls because it is very, very hot, but we have blinds to stop the rain and sun. Our house is in the old style. We have only *one* room for living and sleeping, so it is both a bedroom and a living room. We have rugs and we sit and sleep on the floor.

T 5.6 Asking for directions

1 **A** Excuse me! Is there a chemist near here?
   B Yes. It's over there.
   A Thanks.

2 **A** Excuse me! Is there a newsagent near here?
   B Yes. It's in Church Street. Take the first street on the right. It's next to the music shop.
   A Oh yes. Thanks.

3 **A** Excuse me! Is there a restaurant near here?
   B There's a Chinese one in Park Lane next to the bank, and there's an Italian one in Church Street next to the travel agent.
   A Is that one far?
   B No. Just two minutes, that's all.

4 **A** Is there a post office near here?
   B Go straight ahead, and it's on the left, next to the pub.
   A Thanks a lot.

Unit 6

T 6.1 **What can you do?**

a She can use a computer.
b We can't understand the question.
c 'Can dogs swim?' 'Yes, they can.'
d He can ski really well.
e I can't spell your name.
f 'Can you speak Japanese?' 'No, I can't.'

T 6.2 **Listen and repeat**

I can speak French.
Can you speak French?
Yes, I can.
No, I can't.

T 6.3 **Listen and complete the sentences**

1 I can speak French, but I can't speak
  German.
2 He can't dance, but he can sing.
3 'Can you cook?' 'Yes, I can.'
4 They can ski, but they can't swim.
5 We can dance and we can sing.
6 'Can she drive?' 'No, she can't.'

T 6.4 **Tina can't cook. Can you?**

Well, there are a lot of things I can't do. I can't
drive a car, but I want to have lessons soon. I
can't speak French but I can speak Italian, my
mother's Italian, and we often go to Italy. My
mother's a really good cook, she can cook
really well, not just Italian food, all kinds of
food, but I can't cook at all. I just love eating!
What about sports? Er … I think I'm good at
quite a lot of sports. I can play tennis, and ski,
sometimes we go skiing in the Italian Alps,
and of course I can swim. But musical
instruments – no – I can't play any at all – no
I'm not very musical, but I love dancing! Of
course I can use a computer – all my friends
can.

T 6.5 **Listen and repeat**

It was Monday yesterday. We were at school.
'Was it hot?' 'Yes, it was.'
'Were you tired?' 'Yes, we were.'

T 6.6 **Charlotte's party**

K = Kim   M = Max

K Were you at Charlotte's party last
  Saturday?
M Yes, I was.
K Was it good?
M Well, it was OK.
K Were there many people?
M Yes, there were.
K Was Henry there?
M No, he wasn't. And where were you? Why
  weren't you there?
K Oh … I couldn't go because I was at
  Mark's party! It was brilliant!

T 6.7 **Directory Enquiries**

Operator International Directory Enquiries.
          Which country, please?
Operator And which town?
Operator Can I have the last name, please?
Operator And the initial?
Operator What's the address?
Recorded message The number you require
          is 006198 4681133.

T 6.8 **On the phone**

1 A Hello.
  B Hello. Can I speak to Jo, please?
  A This is Jo.
  B Oh! Hi, Jo. This is Pat. Is Sunday still
    OK for tennis?
  A Yes. That's fine.
  B Great! See you on Sunday at ten, then.
    Bye!
  A Bye!

2 A Hello.
  B Hello. Is that Liz?
  A No it isn't. I'll just get her.
  C Hello, Liz here.
  B Hi, Liz. It's Tom. Listen! There's a party
    at my house on Saturday. Can you
    come?
  C Oh sorry, Tom. I can't. It's my sister's
    wedding.
  B Oh, never mind. Perhaps next time.
    Bye!
  C Bye!

3 A Good morning. Barclays Bank,
    Watford. How can I help you?
  B Good morning. Can I speak to the
    manager, please?
  A I'm afraid Mr Smith isn't in his office at
    the moment. Can I take a message?
  B Don't worry. I'll ring back later.
  A All right. Goodbye.
  B Goodbye.

Unit 7

T 7.1 **Mattie Smith**

Mattie Smith is 91 years old. She lives alone in
Atlanta, Georgia. She starts her day at 7.30.
First she has a bath, next she cleans the house,
and then she sits outside on her verandah and
thinks about her past life. Then she writes
poems about it.

T 7.2 **see p52**

T 7.3 **Listen and repeat**

looked
worked
loved
learned
earned
married
died
hated
wanted

T 7.4 **Listen to Mattie**

I worked from 6.00 in the morning until
10.00 at night. Sixteen hours in the cotton
fields and I only earned $2 a day. I sure hated
that job but I loved the poems in my head. I
really wanted to learn to read and write. When
I was sixteen I married Hubert, and soon
there were six children, five sons, then a
daughter, Lily. Hubert died just before she was
born. That was sixty-five years ago. So I
looked after my family alone. There was no
time for learning, but my children, they all
learned to read and write – that was
important to me. And when did I learn to
read and write? I didn't learn until I was 86,
and now I have three books of poems.

T 7.5 **Questions and answers**

1 A When did she start work?
  B When she was eight years old.
2 A Where did she work?
  B In the cotton fields.
3 A Who did she live with?
  B Her mother and sisters.
4 A How many hours did she work?
  B Sixteen hours a day.
5 A How much did she earn?
  B $2 a day.
6 A Who did she marry?
  B Hubert.
7 A When did Hubert die?
  B Sixty-five years ago.
8 A When did she learn to read?
  B She didn't learn until she was 86.

T 7.6 **Listen carefully!**

worked
lived
started
married
loved
hated
finished
looked
died
visited
cleaned
liked

T 7.7 **Listen and repeat**

had
began
came
went
did
left
got
studied
became
won
lost
bought
met

T 7.8 Simon's 1990s

What do I remember of the nineties … er … well, I left school in 1994 and I went to university. I studied graphic design – it was really good. I had a good time. Then after university, in 1997, I was really lucky. I got a job immediately. A job with Saatchi and Saatchi, they're an advertising agency in London. Soon after that, 1998 it was, I met Zoë, she's my girlfriend. She has a good job, too, and we bought a flat together in 1999.

The only sport I like is football, so I remember when France won the World Cup in 1998. Brazil lost in '98 but they won in '94.

I remember when Tony Blair became Prime Minister in 1997, that was just after I started at Saatchi and Saatchi. Oh, and I remember Bill Clinton and all the problems he had in his last years in the White House. And the Euro – eleven countries in Europe began to use the Euro in 1999, but Britain didn't.

Oh yes – and of course I remember Princess Diana – she died in a car crash in Paris in '97 and millions of people came to London for her funeral. I was there. I can remember it really well.

T 7.9 Listen and repeat

1	walk	7	work
2	listen	8	war
3	know	9	island
4	write	10	build
5	eight	11	resign
6	farm	12	daughter

T 7.10 Listen and repeat

1	born	5	knives
2	bought	6	wrong
3	world	7	cupboard
4	answer	8	Christmas

T 7.11 Special days

1 A Ugh! Work again! I hate Monday mornings!
   B Me, too. Did you have a nice weekend?
   A Yes. It was brilliant.

2 Happy birthday to you.
   Happy birthday to you.
   Happy birthday, dear Tommy,
   Happy birthday to you.

3 A Did you get any Valentine cards?
   B Yes, I did. Listen to this.
      Roses are red. Violets are blue
      You are my Valentine
      And I love you.
   A Oooh-er! Do you know who it's from?
   B No idea!

4 A Congratulations!
   B Oh … thank you very much.
   A When's the happy day?
   B Pardon?
   A Your wedding day. When is it?
   B Oh! We're not sure. Perhaps some time in June.

5 A It's midnight! Happy New Year everybody!
   B Happy New Year !

C Happy New Year !

6 A Thank goodness! It's Friday!
   B Yeah. Have a nice weekend!
   A Same to you.

T 7.12 Listen and answer

1 Did you have a nice weekend?
2 Did you get any Valentine cards?
3 Congratulations!
4 Happy New Year!
5 Have a nice weekend!

Unit 8

T 8.1 Inventions

JEANS
Two Americans, Jacob Davis and Levi Strauss, made the first jeans in 1873. Davis bought cloth from Levi's shop. He told Levi that he had a special way to make strong trousers for workmen. The first jeans were blue. In 1935 jeans became fashionable for women after they saw them in *Vogue* magazine. In the 1970s, Calvin Klein earned $12.5 million a week from jeans.

TELEVISION
A Scotsman, John Logie Baird, transmitted the first television picture on 25 October, 1925. The first thing on television was a boy who worked in the office next to Baird's workroom in London. In 1927 Baird sent pictures from London to Glasgow. In 1928 he sent pictures to New York, and also produced the first colour TV pictures.

ASPIRIN
Felix Hofman a 29-year-old chemist who worked for the German company Bayer, invented the drug Aspirin in March 1899. He gave the first aspirin to his father for his arthritis. By 1950 it was the best-selling painkiller in the world, and in 1969 the Apollo astronauts took it to the moon. The Spanish philosopher, José Ortega y Gasset, called the 20th century 'The Age of Aspirin'.

T 8.2 Negatives and positives

1 Two Germans didn't make the first jeans. Two Americans made them.
2 Davis didn't sell cloth in Levi's shop. He bought cloth from Levi's shop.
3 Women didn't see pictures of jeans in *She* magazine. They saw them in *Vogue*.
4 Baird didn't send pictures from London to Paris. He sent pictures from London to Glasgow.
5 Felix Hofman didn't give the first aspirin to his mother. He gave it to his father.
6 A Spanish philosopher didn't call the 19th century, 'the Age of Aspirin'. He called the 20th century, 'the Age of Aspirin'.

T 8.3 see p62

T 8.4 Listen and repeat

1	recipe	6	worried
2	chat	7	delicious
3	shy	8	sandwich
4	funny	9	machine
5	face	10	century

T 8.5 Everyday conversations

1 A Why didn't you laugh at my joke?
   B Because it wasn't very funny. That's why!

2 A Hello. Hello. I can't hear you. Who is it?
   B It's me, Jonathon … JONATHON! I'm on my mobile phone.
   A Oh, Jonathon! Hi! Sorry, I can't chat now. I'm in a hurry.

3 A Good luck in your exams!
   B Oh, thank you. I always get so nervous before exams.

4 A Mmmmm! Did you make this chocolate cake?
   B I did. Do you like it?
   A Like it? I *love* it. It's delicious. Can I have the recipe?

5 A Come on, Tommy. Say hello to Auntie Mavis. Don't be shy.
   B Hello, Auntie Mavis.

T 8.6

Love on the Internet – Debbie and Per

Debbie I'm really quite shy. I find it difficult to talk to people face to face. But I find it easy to chat on the Internet. I met Per there about a year ago. It was on a chatline called 'the Chat Room'. He was so funny.

Per But I'm only funny on the Internet! Anyway, we chatted on the Internet for a year, we exchanged hundreds of e-mails and some photographs. I wanted to phone Debbie but …

Debbie I said no. I was worried. I didn't want it to end.

Per She didn't even give me her address. But finally she said OK, I could phone, so I did, and we spoke for an hour. It was very expensive! That was six months ago. Then she sent me her address and …

Debbie … that was three months ago and one week later, there was a knock at the door and I knew before I opened it. Somehow I wasn't worried any more. I opened the door and …

Per … and I stood there with some flowers …

Debbie … lots of flowers. Red roses. Beautiful … and …

Per … and well, we fell in love and …

Both … and we got married last Saturday.

Love in a bottle – Rosa and Vincent

Rosa I love the sea. I like walking on the beach. One day, it was five years ago now, I was on the beach and I stood on something, it was a bottle, a green bottle. I could see something inside. Some paper, so I broke the bottle, it was a letter but …

Vincent … but you couldn't read it …

Rosa No, I couldn't. You see it was in English and I couldn't speak English then.

Vincent You can speak it well now …

Rosa No, not really, but anyway. I asked a friend to translate the letter for me. We couldn't believe it. A man in America – he wanted a wife, but the letter was ten years old.

Vincent And I still wasn't married!

Rosa But I didn't know that. Anyway for a joke I wrote and sent a photo …

Vincent And now, I couldn't believe it. I got this letter and a photo. She looked beautiful. I wrote back immediately and we wrote every week for six months … and we spoke on the phone and …

Rosa … and finally I flew to America and we met face to face. I was very shy but it was good, very good and now …

Vincent … now, we have three children. We have a house by the sea …

Rosa We're very happy. You see, we both love the sea!

T 8.7 Ordinals

first
second
third
fourth
fifth
sixth
tenth
twelfth
thirteenth
sixteenth
seventeenth
twentieth
twenty-first
thirtieth
thirty-first

T 8.8 Dates

1 The first of April
  April the first
2 The second of March
  March the second
3 The seventeenth of September
  September the seventeenth
4 The nineteenth of November
  November the nineteenth
5 The twenty-third of June
  June the twenty-third
6 The twenty-ninth of February, nineteen seventy-six
7 The nineteenth of December, nineteen eighty-three

8 The third of October, nineteen ninety-nine
9 The thirty-first of May, two thousand
10 The fifteenth of July, two thousand and four

T 8.9 What's the date?

1 The fourth of January
2 May the seventh, 1997
3 The fifteenth of August, 2001
4 **A** It was a Friday.
  B No, it wasn't. It was a Thursday.
  A No, I remember. It was Friday the thirteenth. The thirteenth of July.
5 **A** Oh no! I forgot your birthday.
  B It doesn't matter, really.
  A It was last Sunday, wasn't it? The thirtieth. November the thirtieth.
6 **A** Hey! Did you know that Shakespeare was born and died on the same day?
  B That's not possible!
  A Yes, it is. He was born on April the twenty-third, fifteen sixty-four and he died on April the twenty-third, sixteen sixteen.

Unit 9

T 9.1 Food you like

D = Daisy   T = Tom
D I don't like tea.
T Oh, I do. Well, sometimes, with sugar. But coffee's horrible!
D Yeah. Disgusting. I don't like wine or beer either.
T Well – I don't like wine but I like beer. My dad has beer every day after work and sometimes I have a bit.
D Beer! Yuk! But apple juice is nice. I really like apple juice. It's delicious.
T Mmmm! Yeah, it's delicious and it's good for you. Apples are too! I love all fruit – apples, oranges, bananas, strawberries.
D Yeah. OK. I like fruit, but I hate all vegetables, 'specially carrots.
T Yeah, vegetables are disgusting. Er – but not all of them, – I quite like peas. Hamburgers, chips, and peas. Mmm! That's one of my favourite meals.
D Yeah – hamburgers, I like. Chips, I like. But peas – yuk!
T My very favourite meal is spaghetti. Spaghetti, then ice-cream after. Yummy! … Or yoghurt. I love strawberry yoghurt.
D Ice-cream – OK, yes. Yoghurt, no! Spaghetti – yes. I like all pasta and pizza! But I don't like it with tomatoes or cheese. I don't like tomatoes very much and I hate cheese.
T Mmmm! Pizza. The best. But … you can't have pizza without tomatoes and cheese.
D You can.
T You can't!
D Can!
T Can't!
D Well, I can. I don't like cheese at all!

T What do you like then?
D Well, I like … er … I like chocolate and chocolate biscuits …
T Yeah! I really like chocolate. Everybody likes chocolate.
D Yeah!

T 9.2 see p67

T 9.3 Questions and answers

1 Would you like a cigarette?
  No, thanks. I don't smoke.
2 Do you like your teacher?
  Yes. She's very nice.
3 Would you like a drink?
  Yes, please. Some Coke, please.
4 Can I help you?
  Yes. I'd like a book of stamps, please.
5 What sports do you do?
  Well, I like swimming very much.
6 Excuse me, are you ready to order?
  Yes. I'd like a steak, please.

T 9.4 Listen carefully!

1 Good afternoon. Can I help you?
2 Who's your favourite writer?
3 What would you like for your birthday?
4 Do you like animals?
5 Here's the wine list, sir.
6 Have some ice-cream with your strawberries.

T 9.5

1 **A** Good afternoon. Can I help you?
  B Yes. I'd like some fruit, please.
2 **A** Who's your favourite writer?
  B I like books by John Grisham.
3 **A** What would you like for your birthday?
  B I'd like a new bike.
4 **A** Do you like animals?
  B I like cats, but I don't like dogs.
5 **A** Here's the wine list, sir.
  B We'd like a bottle of French red wine.
6 **A** Have some ice-cream with your strawberries.
  B No, thanks. I don't like ice-cream.

T 9.6 Going shopping

B = Barry   MP = Miss Potts
MP Good morning. Can I help you?
B Yes. I'd like some orange juice, please.
MP Er … sorry. There's apple juice but no orange juice.
B What's that then? Isn't that orange juice?
MP Oh, yes. So it is! My eyes! Here you are.
B Thank you, and some milk, please.
MP Sorry. I sold the last bottle two minutes ago.
B Oh, dear! What about some coffee?
MP Yes. Here you are.
B Thanks. That's orange juice, coffee … er … and … er … a kilo of apples, please.
MP I don't sell apples.
B You don't sell apples! That's strange. What about cheese. Can I have some cheese?
MP I don't sell cheese, either.

B You don't sell cheese! That's amazing. Now, I want some pizza, but I'm sure you don't sell pizza, do you?

MP Oh, yes I do. What would you like? Pizza with mushrooms, pizza with cheese and ham, pizza with sausage, or pizza with tomatoes?

B Wow! Can I have … er … some pizza with cheese and tomatoes, please?

MP Oh, sorry. I forgot. Usually, I have pizza but not on Thursdays. Today's Thursday, isn't it?

B Yes, it is. Mmm … OK, … er … OK, forget the pizza. What about bread? I don't suppose you have any bread?

MP Yes, you're right.

B Pardon?

MP You're right. There isn't any bread.

B Tell me. Do you do a lot of business?

MP Oh, yes sir. This shop is open 24 hours.

B Really! What do people buy?

MP All the things you see.

B Mmmm. OK. That's all for me. How much?

MP That's £5.60, please.

B Thank you. Goodbye.

MP Goodbye sir. See you again soon.

B I don't think so.

T 9.7 **My favourite food**

Marian

Well, I love vegetables, all vegetables – I eat meat too – but not much. I think this is why I like Chinese food so much. There are lots of vegetables in Chinese food. Yes, Chinese is my very favourite food, I like the noodles too. Can you eat with chopsticks? I can!

Graham

Now in my job, I travel the world, and I like all kinds of food … but my favourite, my favourite is … er … I always have it as soon as I come home … is a full English breakfast. Bacon, eggs, sausage, mushrooms, tomatoes, and of course toast. I love it, not every day but when I'm at home we have it every Sunday. Mmmm! I'd like it right now – delicious.

Lucy

Oh, no question, no problem. I know exactly what my favourite food is. Pasta. All pasta. Especially spaghetti. Pasta with tomato sauce – and I like it best when I'm in Italy. I went on holiday to the Italian lakes last year. The food was wonderful.

Gavin

… er … I'm not sure. No, I know what it is. My … favourite … food is Indian food. Friday night I like to go to the pub with friends from work and … have a few beers, … er … no, not too many, … and after we always go to an Indian restaurant and I have a chicken curry with rice. It's the best! I like it more than chips!

Sally

Well, shhh! But my very, very favourite food is chocolate. Chocolate anything, I love it. Chocolate ice-cream, chocolate biscuits, chocolate cake, but especially just a big bar of chocolate. Mmmm! Terrible, isn't it? Go on! Have some of this! My friend brought it back from Switzerland for me!

T 9.8 **Polite requests**

1 Would you like some more carrots?
Yes, please. They're delicious.
2 Could you pass the salt, please?
Yes, of course. Here you are.
3 Could I have a glass of water, please?
Do you want fizzy or still?
4 Does anybody want more dessert?
Yes, please. I'd love some. It's delicious.
5 How would you like your coffee?
Black, no sugar, please.
6 This is delicious! Can you give me the recipe?
Yes, of course. I'm glad you like it.
7 Do you want help with the washing-up?
No, of course not. We have a dishwasher.

T 9.9

1 Can I have a cheese sandwich, please?
Yes, of course. That's £1.75.
2 Could you tell me the time, please?
It's just after ten.
3 Can you take me to school?
Jump in.
4 Can I see the menu, please?
Here you are. And would you like a drink to start?
5 Could you lend me some money, please?
Not again! How much would you like this time?
6 Can you help me with my homework, please?
What is it? French? I can't speak a word of French.
7 Can I borrow your dictionary, please?
Yes, if I can find it. I think it's in my bag.

Unit 10

T 10.1 **Listen and repeat**

The country is cheaper and safer than the city.
The city is noisier and dirtier than the country.
The city is more expensive than the country.
The city is more exciting than the country.

T 10.2 **Much more than …**

1 **A** Life in the country is slower than city life.
  B Yes, the city's much faster.
2 **A** New York is safer than London.
  B No, it isn't. New York is much more dangerous.
3 **A** Paris is bigger than Madrid.
  B No, it isn't! It's much smaller.

4 **A** Madrid is more expensive than Rome.
  B No, it isn't. Madrid is much cheaper.
5 **A** The buildings in Rome are more modern than the buildings in New York.
  B No, they aren't. They're much older.
6 **A** The Underground in London is better than the Metro in Paris.
  B No! The Underground is much worse.

T 10.3 **Mel's got a better job**

Tara Why did you leave London? You had a good job.

Mel Yes, but I've got a better job here.

Tara And you had a big flat in London.

Mel Well, I've got a bigger flat here.

Tara Really? How many bedrooms has it got?

Mel Three. And it's got a garden. It's nicer than my flat in London and it's cheaper.

Tara But you haven't got any friends!

Mel I've got a lot of friends here. People are much friendlier than in London.

Tara But the country's so boring.

Mel No, it isn't. It's much more exciting than London. Seacombe has got shops, a cinema, a theatre, and a park. And the air is cleaner and the streets are safer.

Tara OK. Everything is wonderful! So when can I visit you?

T 10.4 **The biggest and best!**

1 That house is very big.
Yes, it's the biggest house in the village.
2 Claridge's is a very expensive hotel.
Yes, it's the most expensive hotel in London.
3 Castle Combe is a very pretty village.
Yes, it's the prettiest village in England.
4 New York is a very cosmopolitan city.
Yes, it's the most cosmopolitan city in the world.
5 Tom Hanks is a very popular film star.
Yes, he's the most popular film star in America.
6 Miss Smith is a very funny teacher.
Yes, she's the funniest teacher in our school.
7 Anna is a very intelligent student.
Yes, she's the most intelligent student in the class.
8 This is a very easy exercise.
Yes, it's the easiest exercise in the book.

T 10.5 **Listen and respond**

1 That house is very big.
2 Claridge's is a very expensive hotel.
3 Castle Combe is a very pretty village.
4 New York is a very cosmopolitan city.
5 Tom Hanks is a very popular film star.
6 Miss Smith is a very funny teacher.
7 Anna is a very intelligent student.
8 This is a very easy exercise.

T 10.6 **A musical interlude**

(three music excerpts)

T 10.7 Listen and repeat

wood
theatre
farm
village
factory
cottage
field
church

T 10.8 To the lake

Drive along Park Road and turn right. Go under the bridge and past the pub. Turn left up the hill, then drive down the hill to the river. Turn right after the farm and the lake is on the right. It takes twenty minutes.

T 10.9 A drive in the country

Well, I drove out of the garage, along the road, and under the bridge. Then I drove past the pub, up the hill, and down the hill. But then I drove over the river, and then – it was terrible – I went through the hedge, and into the lake!

Unit 11

T 11.1 Who's at the party?

O = Oliver   M = Monica

O   Oh dear! Monica, I don't know any of these people. Who are they?

M   Don't worry Oliver. They're all very nice. Can you see that man over there? He's sitting down. That's Harry. He's a musician. He works in LA.

O   Sorry, where?

M   You know, LA. Los Angeles.

O   Oh yeah.

M   And he's talking to Mandy. She's wearing a red dress. She's very nice and very rich! She lives in a beautiful old house in the country.

O   Rich, eh?

M   Yes. Rich and married! Next to her is Fiona. She's drinking a glass of red wine. Fiona's my oldest friend, she and I were at school together.

O   And what does Fiona do?

M   She's a writer. She writes children's stories – they're not very good but … anyway, she's talking to George. He's laughing and smoking a cigar. He's a pilot. He travels the world, thousands of miles every week.

O   And who are those two over there? They're dancing. Mmmm. They know each other very well.

M   Oh, that's Roz and Sam. They're married. They live in the flat upstairs.

O   So … er … that's Harry and Mandy and … er … it's no good, I can't remember all those names.

T 11.2 Listen to the questions

1   Whose is the baseball cap?
2   Whose are the roller blades?
3   Whose is the dog?

T 11.3 *who's* or *whose*?

1   Who's on the phone?
2   I'm going to the pub. Who's coming?
3   Wow! Look at that sports car. Whose is it?
4   Whose dictionary is this? It's not mine.
5   There are books all over the floor. Whose are they?
6   Who's the most intelligent in our class?
7   Who's got my book?
8   Do you know whose jacket this is?

T 11.4 What a mess!

A   Whose is this tennis racket?
B   It's mine.
A   What's it doing here?
B   I'm playing tennis this afternoon.

T 11.5 What a wonderful world

I see trees of green
Red roses too
I see them bloom for me and you
And I think to myself
what a wonderful world.
I see skies of blue
and clouds of white
the bright sunny day
and the dark starry night
and I think to myself
what a wonderful world
The colours of the rainbow
so pretty in the sky
are also on the faces
of the people going by.
I see friends shaking hands
saying 'How do you do?'
They're really saying
'I love you.'
I hear babies cry
I watch them grow.
They'll learn much more
than you'll ever know
and I think to myself
what a wonderful world.
Yes, I think to myself
what a wonderful world.

T 11.6 Vowels and diphthongs

Vowels

1	red	said
2	hat	that
3	kissed	list
4	green	mean
5	laugh	half
6	whose	shoes
7	short	bought

Diphthongs

1	white	night
2	near	beer
3	they	pay
4	hair	wear
5	rose	knows
6	ours	flowers

T 11.7 Tongue twisters

1   Four fine fresh fish for you.
2   Six silly sisters selling shiny shoes.

3   If a dog chews shoes, whose shoes does he choose?
4   I'm looking back,
    To see if she's looking back,
    To see if I'm looking back,
    To see if she's looking back at me!

T 11.8 In a clothes shop

SA = shop assistant   C = customer

SA   Can I help you?

C   Yes, please. I'm looking for a shirt to go with my new suit.

SA   What colour are you looking for?

C   Blue.

SA   What about this one? Do you like this?

C   No, it isn't the right blue.

SA   Well, what about this one? It's a bit darker blue.

C   Oh yes. I like that one much better. Can I try it on?

SA   Yes, of course. The changing rooms are over there.
     Is the size OK?

C   No, it's a bit too big. Have you got a smaller size?

SA   That's the last blue one we've got, I'm afraid. But we've got it in white.

C   OK. I'll take the white. How much is it?

SA   £39.99. How do you want to pay?

C   Can I pay by credit card?

SA   Credit card's fine. Thank you very much.

Unit 12

T 12.1

Rosie

When I grow up I'm going to be a ballet dancer. I love dancing. I go dancing three times a week. I'm going to travel all over the world and I'm going to learn French and Russian because I want to dance in Paris and Moscow. I'm not going to marry until I'm thirty-five and then I'm going to have two children. First I'd like a girl and then a boy – but maybe I can't plan that! I'm going to work until I'm 75. I'm going to teach dancing and I'm going to open a dance school. It's all very exciting.

Miss Bishop

When I retire … ? … er … well … er … two things. First, I'm going to learn Russian – I can already speak French and German, and I want to learn another language. And second, I'm going to learn to drive. It's terrible that I'm 59 and I can't drive – no time to learn. Then I'm going to buy a car and travel all over the world. Also I'm not going to wear boring clothes any more, I hate the skirts and blouses I wear every day for school. I'm going to wear jeans and T-shirts all the time. And when I return from my travels I'm going to write a book and go on TV to talk about it. I'm going to become a TV star!

T 12.2 **Listen and repeat**

A Is she going to be a ballet dancer?
B Yes, she is.
A What's she going to do?
B Travel all over the world.

T 12.3 **Questions about Rosie**

1 A Why is she going to learn French and Russian?
  B Because she wants to dance in Paris and Moscow.
2 A When is she going to marry?
  B Not until she's thirty-five.
3 A How many children is she going to have?
  B Two.
4 A How long is she going to work?
  B Until she's seventy-five.
5 A What is she going to teach?
  B Dancing.

T 12.4 **It's going to rain**

1 Take an umbrella. It's going to rain.
2 Look at the time! You're going to be late for the meeting.
3 Anna's running very fast. She's going to win the race.
4 Look! Jack's on the wall. He's going to fall.
5 Look at that man! He's going to jump.
6 They're going to have a baby. It's due next month.
7 There's my sister and her boyfriend! Yuk! They're going to kiss.
8 'Oh dear. I'm going to sneeze. Aaattishooo!'
  'Bless you!'

T 12.5 **Why are you going?**

MB = Miss Bishop   H = Harold
MB First I'm going to Holland.
H Why?
MB To see the tulips, of course!
H Oh yes! How wonderful! Where are you going after that?
MB Well, then I'm going to Spain to watch flamenco dancing.

T 12.6 **The weather**

A What's the weather like today?
B It's snowy and it's very cold.
A What was it like yesterday?
B Oh, it was cold and cloudy.
A What's it going to be like tomorrow?
B I think it's going to be warmer.

T 12.7 **Conversations about the weather**

1 A It's a lovely day! What shall we do?
  B Let's play tennis!
2 A It's raining again! What shall we do?
  B Let's stay at home and watch a video.

T 12.8

1 A It's a lovely day! What shall we do?
  B Let's play tennis!
  A Oh no! It's too hot to play tennis.
  B Well, let's go to the beach.
  A OK. I'll get my swimming costume.

2 A It's raining again! What shall we do?
  B Let's stay at home and watch a video.
  A Oh no! We watched a video last night.
  B Well, let's go to the cinema.
  A OK. Which film do you want to see?

Unit 13

T 13.1 **A general knowledge quiz**

1 When did the first man walk on the moon?
  In 1969.
2 Where are the Andes mountains?
  In South America.
3 Who did Mother Teresa look after?
  Poor people in Calcutta.
4 Who won the last World Cup?
  France in 1998.
5 How many American states are there?
  50.
6 How much does an African elephant weigh?
  5–7 tonnes.
7 How far is it from London to New York?
  6,000 kilometres.
8 How old was Princess Diana when she died?
  36.
9 What languages do Swiss people speak?
  German, French, Italian, and Romansch.
10 What did Marconi invent in 1901?
  The radio.
11 What sort of music did Louis Armstrong play?
  Jazz.
12 What happens at the end of *Romeo and Juliet*?
  Romeo and Juliet kill themselves.
13 What happened in Europe in 1939?
  The Second World War started.
14 Why do birds migrate?
  Because the winter is cold.
15 Which was the first country to have TV?
  Britain.
16 Which language has the most words?
  English.

T 13.2 **Listen carefully!**

1 Why do you want to go?
2 Who is she?
3 Where's he staying?
4 Why didn't they come?
5 How old was she?
6 Does he play the guitar?
7 Where did you go at the weekend?

T 13.3 **Noises in the night**

It was about 2 o'clock in the morning, and … suddenly I woke up. I heard a noise. I got out of bed and went slowly downstairs. There was a light on in the living room. I listened carefully. I could hear two men speaking very quietly. 'Burglars!' I thought. 'Two burglars!' Immediately I ran back upstairs and phoned the police. I was really frightened. Fortunately the police arrived quickly. They opened the front door and went into the living room. Then they came upstairs to find me. 'It's all right now, sir,' they explained. 'We turned the television off for you!'

T 13.4 see p102

T 13.5 see p104

T 13.6 **Catching a train**

Trains from Oxford to Bristol Temple Meads.
Monday to Friday.
Here are the departure times from Oxford and arrival times in Bristol.

0816 arriving 0946
0945 arriving 1114
1040 arriving 1208
11…

T 13.7 **The information bureau**

A = Ann   B = clerk
A Good morning. Can you tell me the times of trains from Bristol back to Oxford, please?
B Afternoon, evening? When do you want to come back?
A About five o'clock this afternoon.
B About five o'clock. Right. Let's have a look. There's a train that leaves at 5.28, then there isn't another one until 6.50.
A And what time do they get in?
B The 5.28 gets into Oxford at 6.54 and the 6.50 gets in at 8.10.
A Thanks a lot.

T 13.8 **At the ticket office**

A Hello. A return to Bristol, please.
C Day return or period return?
A A day return.
C How do you want to pay?
A Cash, please.
C That's eighteen pounds.
A Here's a twenty-pound note.
C Here's your change and your ticket.
A Thank you. Which platform is it?
C You want platform 1 over there.
A OK, thanks very much. Goodbye.

Unit 14

T 14.1 see p106

T 14.2 see p106

T 14.3 **The life of Ryan**

Yes, I've lived in a foreign country. In Japan, actually. I lived in Osaka for a year. I enjoyed it very much. I loved the food. And, yes, I have worked for a big company. I worked for Nissan, the car company, that's why I was in Japan. That was two years ago, then I got another job.
  Have I stayed in an expensive hotel? No, never – only cheap hotels for me, I'm afraid, but I have flown in a jumbo jet – four or five times, actually. Oh, I've never cooked a meal

for a lot of people. I love food but I don't like cooking, sometimes I cook for me and my girlfriend but she likes it better if we go out for a meal! And I've never met a famous person – oh, just a minute, well not met but I've seen … er… I saw a famous politician at the airport once – Oh, who was it? I can't remember his name. Er … I've only seen one Shakespeare play, when I was at school, we saw *Romeo and Juliet*. It was OK. I've driven a tractor though, I had a holiday job on a farm when I was 17. I enjoyed that. Good news – I've never been to hospital. I was born in hospital, of course, but that's different. Bad news – I've never won a competition. I do the lottery every week but I've never, ever won a thing!

T 14.4 **A honeymoon in London**

M = Marilyn   J = Judy

M We're having a great time!

J Tell me about it! What have you done so far?

M Well, we've been to Buckingham Palace. That was the first thing we did. It's right in the centre of London! We went inside and looked around.

J Have you seen the Houses of Parliament yet?

M Yeah, we have. We've just had a boat ride on the River Thames and we went right past the Houses of Parliament. We saw Big Ben! Then we went on the London Eye. That's the big wheel near Big Ben. That was this morning. This afternoon we're going to take a taxi to Hyde Park and then go shopping in Harrods. Tomorrow morning we're going to see the Crown Jewels in the Tower of London.

J Wow! You're busy! And what about those big red buses? Have you travelled on a double-decker bus yet?

M Oh, yeah we took one when we went to Buckingham Palace. We sat upstairs. You get a great view of the city.

J Tomorrow's your last night. What are you going to do on your last night?

M Well, we're going to the theatre, but we haven't decided what to see yet.

J Oh, you're so lucky! Give my love to Rod!

M Yeah. Bye, Judy. See you soon!

T 14.5 **Leaving on a jet plane**

My bags are packed, I'm ready to go
I'm standing here outside your door,
I hate to wake you up to say goodbye
But the dawn is breaking,
It's early morn'
The taxi's waiting,
He's blowing his horn.
Already I'm so lonesome
I could die.

So kiss me and smile for me,
Tell me that you'll wait for me,
Hold me like you'll never let me go,
'Cos I'm leaving on a jet plane,
I don't know when I'll be back again.
Oh babe, I hate to go.

There's so many times I've let you down,
So many times I've played around,
I tell you now
They don't mean a thing.
Every place I go, I'll think of you
Every song I sing, I'll sing for you
When I come back
I'll wear your wedding ring.

T 14.6 **Flight information**

British Airways flight BA 516 to Geneva boarding at gate 4, last call. Flight BA 516 to Geneva, last call. Scandinavian Airlines flight SK 832 to Frankfurt is delayed one hour. Flight SK 832 to Frankfurt, delayed one hour. Air France flight 472 to Amsterdam is now boarding at gate 17. Flight AF 472 to Amsterdam, now boarding, gate 17. Lufthansa flight 309 to Miami is now boarding at gate 32. Flight LH 309 to Miami, now boarding, gate 32. Virgin Airlines flight to New York, VS 876 to New York. Please wait in the departure lounge until a further announcement. Thank you. Passengers are reminded to keep their hand luggage with them at all times.

T 14.7 **Conversations at the airport**

1 **A** Listen! … BA 516 to Geneva. That's our flight.

  B Did the announcement say gate 4 or 14?

  A I couldn't hear. I think it said 4.

  B Look! There it is on the departure board. It *is* gate 4.

  A OK. Come on! Let's go.

2 **A** Can I have your ticket, please?

  B Yes, of course.

  A Thank you. How many suitcases have you got?

  B Just one.

  A And have you got much hand luggage?

  B Just this bag.

  A That's fine.

  B Oh … can I have a seat next to the window?

  A Yes, that's OK. Here's your boarding pass. Have a nice flight!

3 **A** Rod! Marilyn! Over here!

  B Hi! Judy! Great to see you!

  A It's great to see you too. You look terrific! Did you have a good honeymoon?

  B Fantastic. Everything was fantastic.

  A Well, you haven't missed anything here. Nothing much has happened at all!

4 **A** There's my flight. It's time to go.

  B Oh no! It's been a wonderful two weeks. I can't believe it's over.

  A I know. When can we see each other again?

  B Soon, I hope. I'll write every day.

  A I'll phone too. Goodbye.

  B Goodbye. Give my love to your family.

Grammar Reference

Unit 1

1.1 Verb *to be*

Positive

I	am			I'm = I am
He She It	is	from the USA.		He's = He is She's = She is It's = It is
We You They	are			We're = We are You're = You are They're = They are

Question

	am	I	
Where	is	he she it	from?
	are	we you they	

I'm 20

I'm 20.	NOT	I'm 20 years.
I'm 20 years old.		I have 20 years.

1.2 Possessive adjectives

What's	my your his	name?	What's = What is
This is	her its our your their	house.	

1.3 Question words

What is your phone number?
Where are you from?
How are you?

1.4 *a/an*

It's a	ticket. newspaper. magazine.

We use *an* before a vowel.

It's an	apple. envelope. English dictionary.

I'm a doctor.	NOT	I'm doctor.
I'm a student.		I'm student.

1.5 Plural nouns

1 Most nouns add *-s* in the plural.
   stamp**s**
   key**s**
   camera**s**

2 If the noun ends in *-s, -ss, -sh,* or *-ch*, add *-es*.

bus	bus**es**
class	class**es**
wish	wish**es**
match	match**es**

3 If the noun ends in a consonant + *-y*, the y changes to *-ies*.

country	countr**ies**
party	part**ies**

But if the noun ends in a vowel + *-y*, the *-y* doesn't change.

key	key**s**
day	day**s**

4 Some nouns are irregular. Dictionaries show this.

child	children
person	people
woman	women
man	men

1.6 Numbers 1–20

1	one
2	two
3	three
4	four
5	five
6	six
7	seven
8	eight
9	nine
10	ten
11	eleven
12	twelve
13	thirteen
14	fourteen
15	fifteen
16	sixteen
17	seventeen
18	eighteen
19	nineteen
20	twenty

1.7 Prepositions

Where are you **from**?
I live **in** a house **in** Toluca.
What's this **in** English?

Unit 2

2.1 Verb *to be*

Questions with question words

What	is her surname? is his job? is her address?		Anderson. He's a policeman. 34, Church Street.
Where	is she are you are they	from?	Mexico.
Who	is Lara? is she?		She's Patrick's daughter.
How old	is he? are you?		Twenty-two.
How much	is an ice-cream?		One pound 50p.

Answers (shown in the right column above)

Yes/No questions — **Short answers**

Is	he she it	hot?	Yes, he is. No, she isn't. Yes, it is.
Are	you they	married?	No, I'm not./No, we aren't. Yes, they are./No, they aren't.

Negative

I	'm not		I'm not = I am not (~~I amn't~~)
He She It	isn't	from the States.	He isn't = He is not She isn't = She is not It isn't = It is not
We You They	aren't		We aren't = We are not You aren't = You are not They aren't = They are not

2.2 Possessive *'s*

My wife**'s** name is Judy.
That's Andrea**'s** dictionary.

2.3 Numbers 21–100

21 twenty-one
22 twenty-two
23 twenty-three
24 twenty-four
25 twenty-five
26 twenty-six
27 twenty-seven
28 twenty-eight
29 twenty-nine
30 thirty
31 thirty-one
40 forty
50 fifty
60 sixty
70 seventy
80 eighty
90 ninety
100 one hundred

2.4 Prepositions

This is a photo **of** my family.
It's good practice **for** you.

I'm **at** home. My mother and father are **at** work.
I'm **at** La Guardia Community College.

I'm **in** New York. I'm **in** a class **with** eight other students.
I live **in** an apartment **with** two American girls.
Central Park is lovely **in** the snow.

Unit 3

3.1 Present Simple *he, she, it*

1 The Present Simple expresses a fact which is always true, or true for a long time.

He **comes** from Switzerland.
She **works** in a bank.

2 It also expresses a habit.

She **goes** skiing in winter.
He never **has** a holiday.

Positive

He She It	lives	in Australia.

Have is irregular.   She **has** a dog.   NOT   she ~~haves~~

Negative

He She It	doesn't live	in France.	doesn't = does not

Question

Where does	he she it	live?

Yes/No **questions**   **Short answers**

Does	he she it	live	in Australia?	Yes, he does. No, she doesn't.
			in France?	Yes, it does.

3.2 Spelling of the third person singular

1 Most verbs add *-s* in the third person singular.

wear	wears
speak	speaks
live	lives

But *go* and *do* are different. They add *-es*.

go	goes
do	does

2 If the verb ends in *-s*, *-sh*, or *-ch*, add *-es*.

finish	finishes
watch	watches

3 If the verb ends in a consonant + *-y*, the *y* changes to *-ies*.

fly	flies
study	studies

But if the verb ends in a vowel + *-y* the *y* does not change.

play	plays

4 *Have* is irregular.

have	has

3.3 Prepositions

She lives **in** Switzerland.
She goes skiing **in** her free time.
In the evening we have supper.
A nurse looks **after** people **in** hospital.
She likes going **for** walks **in** summer.

Get **on** the bus.
He lives **on** an island **in** the west of Scotland.

He collects the post **from** the boat.
He delivers the beer **to** the pub.
He drives the children **to** school.
At ten we go **to** bed.
He likes listening **to** music.
He speaks **to** people **on** his radio.
She's married **to** an American.

There's a letter **for** you.
He makes breakfast **for** the guests.
He writes **for** a newspaper.

He works **as** an undertaker.
Tourists come **by** boat.
It's **about** 6.30.

Unit 4

4.1 Present Simple

Positive

I You We They	start	
He She It	starts	at 6.30.

Negative

I You We They	don't		
He She It	doesn't	start	at 6.30.

Question

When	do	I you we they	start?
	does	he she it	

Yes/No questions

Do	you they	have	a camera?
Does	he she it	like	Chinese food?

Short answers

No, I don't./No, we don't.
Yes, they do.

Yes, he does.
No, she doesn't.
Yes, it does.

4.2 Adverbs of frequency

0%		50%		100%
never	sometimes	often	usually	always

1 These adverbs usually come before the main verb.
   I **usually** go to bed at about 11.00.
   I don't **often** go swimming.
   She **never** eats meat.
   We **always** have wine in the evenings.
   I **sometimes** play tennis on Saturdays.

2 *Sometimes* and *usually* can also come at the beginning or the end of a sentence.
   Sometimes we play cards.   We play cards **sometimes**.
   Usually I walk to school.   I walk to school **usually**.

3 *Never* and *always* can't come at the beginning or the end of a sentence.
   NOT   ~~Never I go to the theatre.~~
          ~~Always I have tea in the morning.~~

4.3 *like/love* + verb + *-ing*

When *like* and *love* are followed by a verb, it is usually verb + *-ing*.
   I **like** cook**ing**.
   She **loves** listen**ing** to music.
   They **like** sail**ing** very much.

4.4 Prepositions

She gets up early **on** weekdays.
He plays football **on** Friday mornings.
They never go out **on** Friday evenings.
Where do you go **on** holiday?
He lives **on** the next block.
He hates watching football **on** television.

Do you relax **at** weekends?
She gets up **at** six o'clock.

She gets up early **in** the morning.
We go out **in** the evening.
He takes photos **in** (the) spring.

Unit 5

5.1 *There is/are*

Positive

There	is	a sofa.	(singular)
	are	two books.	(plural)

Negative

There	isn't	an armchair.	(singular)
	aren't	any flowers.	(plural)

Yes/No questions

Is	there	a table?
Are		any photos?

Short answers

Yes, there is.
No, there isn't.

Yes, there are.
No, there aren't.

5.2 *How many . . . ?*

How many books do you have?

5.3 *some/any*

Positive
There are **some** flowers.   *some* + plural noun

Negative
There aren't **any** cups.   *any* + plural noun

Question
Are there **any** books?   *any* + plural noun

5.4 this, that, these, those

We use *this* and *these* to talk about people/things that are near to us.
> I like **this** ice-cream.
> I want **these** shoes.

We use *that* and *those* to talk about people/things that aren't near to us.
> Do you like **that** picture on the wall?
> Who are **those** children outside?

5.5 Prepositions

> It's the best home **in** the world.
> The front door is **at** the top of the steps.
> There are magazines **under** the table.

> There is a photo **on** the television.
> There are two pictures **on** the wall.
> The cinema is **on** the left, **opposite** the flower shop.

> The bank is **next to** the supermarket.
> The bus stop is **near** the park.
> There is a post box **in front of** the chemist's.

Unit 6

6.1 can/can't

Can and *can't* have the same form in all persons.
There is no *do* or *does*.
Can is followed by the infinitive (without *to*).

could/couldn't

Could is the past of *can*. *Could* and *couldn't* have the same form in all persons.
Could is followed by the infinitive (without *to*).

Positive

I He/She/It We You They	can could	swim.

Negative

I He/She/It We You They	can't couldn't	dance.

NOT   He ~~doesn't can~~ dance.

Question

What	can could	I you he/she/it we they	do?

Yes/No questions

Can Could	you she they	drive? cook?

Short answers

No, I can't./No, we couldn't.
Yes, she can/could.
Yes, they can/could.

NOT   ~~Do you can~~ drive?

6.2 was/were

Was/were is the past of *am/is/are*.

Positive

I He/She/It	was	in Paris yesterday. in England last year.
We You They	were	

Negative

I He/She/It	wasn't	at school yesterday. at the party last night.
We You They	weren't	

Question

Where	was	I? he/she/it?
	were	we? you? they?

Yes/No questions

Was	he she	at work? at home?
Were	you they	

Short answers

No, he wasn't.
Yes, she was.

Yes, I was./Yes, we were.
No, they weren't.

was born

Where	was	she he	born?
	were	you they	

I **was born** in Manchester in 1980.   NOT   ~~I am born~~ in 1980.

6.3 Prepositions

> They were **in** England in 1998.
> I was **at** a party.
> Yesterday there was a party **at** my house.
> Can I speak **to** you?
> She sells pictures **for** $10,000.
> She paints **for** two hours **until** bedtime.

Unit 7

7.1 Past Simple – spelling of regular verbs

1 The normal rule is to add -ed.
    work**ed**   start**ed**
 If the verb ends in -e, add -d.
    live**d**   love**d**

2 If the verb has only one syllable and one vowel and one consonant, double the consonant.
    sto**pp**ed   plan**n**ed

3 Verbs that end in a consonant + -y change to -ied.
    stud**ied**   carr**ied**

7.2 Past Simple

The Past Simple expresses a past action that is finished.
    I **lived** in Rome when I was 6.
    She **started** work when she was 8.
The form of the Past Simple is the same in all persons.

Positive

I He/She/It We You They	moved went	to London in 1985.

Negative
We use *didn't* + infinitive (without *to*) in all persons.

I He/She/It We You They	didn't	move go	to London.

Question
We use *did* + infinitive (without *to*) in all persons.

When Where	did	I you he/she/it we they	go?

Yes/No questions

Did	you she they etc.	like enjoy	the film? the party?

Short answers

No, I didn't./No, we didn't.
Yes, she did.
No, they didn't.

There is list of irregular verbs on p142.

7.3 Time expressions

last	night Saturday week month year
yesterday	morning afternoon evening

7.4 Prepositions

She thinks **about** her past life.
She died **in** a car crash.
He was tired **of** politics.
People were afraid **of** her.
Politics was the love **of** her life.
Who is the card **from**?
She worked **from** 6.00 **until** 10.00.

Unit 8

8.1 Past Simple

Negative
Negatives in the Past Simple are the same in all persons.

I He/She We You They	didn't	go out see Tom watch TV	last night.

ago

I went to the USA	ten years two weeks a month	ago.

8.2 Time expressions

in	the twentieth century 1924 the 1990s winter/summer the evening/the morning September
on	10 October Christmas Day Saturday Sunday evening
at	seven o'clock weekends night

8.3 Prepositions

What's **on** television this evening?
I'm **on** a mobile phone.
We spoke for an hour **on** the phone.
Some people try to find love **on** the internet.
We didn't laugh **at** his joke.
There was a knock **at** the door.
Today's the third **of** April.

Unit 9

9.1 Count and uncount nouns

Some nouns are countable.
    a book   two books
    an egg   six eggs
Some nouns are uncountable.
    bread   rice
Some nouns are both!
    Do you like ice-cream?
    We'd like three ice-creams, please.

9.2 *would like*

Would is the same in all persons. We use *would like* in offers and requests.

Positive

I You He/She/It We They	'd like	a drink.	'd = would

Yes/No questions

Would	you he/she/it they	like a biscuit?

Short answers

Yes, please.
No, thank you.

9.3 *some* and *any*

We use *some* in positive sentences with uncountable nouns and plural nouns.

There is	some	bread	on the table.
There are		oranges	

We use *some* in questions when we ask for things and offer things.

Can I have	some	coffee, please?	(I know there is some coffee.)
Would you like		grapes?	(I know there are some grapes.)

We use *any* in questions and negative sentences with uncountable nouns and plural nouns.

Is there	any	water?	(I don't know if there is any water.)
Does she have		children?	(I don't know if she has any children.)
I can't see		rice.	
There aren't		people.	

9.4 *How much . . . ?* and *How many . . . ?*

We use *How much . . . ?* with uncount nouns.
    How much rice is there?
    There isn't much rice.
We use *How many . . . ?* with count nouns.
    How many apples are there?
    There aren't many apples.

9.5 Prepositions

I've got a book **by** John Grisham.
Help me **with** my homework.

Unit 10

10.1 Comparative and superlative adjectives

	Adjective	Comparative	Superlative
One-syllable adjectives	old safe big hot	old**er** safe**r** big**ger** hot**ter**	the old**est** the safe**st** the big**gest*** the hot**test***
Adjectives ending in -y	nois**y** dirt**y**	nois**ier** dirt**ier**	the nois**iest** the dirt**iest**
Adjectives with two or more syllables	boring beautiful	**more** boring **more** beautiful	the **most** boring the **most** beautiful
Irregular adjectives	good bad far	**better** **worse** **further**	the **best** the **worst** the **furthest**

* Adjectives which end in one vowel and one consonant double the consonant.

> You're **older than** me.
> New York is **dirtier than** Paris.
> Prague is one of **the most beautiful** cities in Europe.

10.2 *have got* and *have*

Have got means the same as *have* to talk about possession, but the form is very different. We often use *have got* in spoken English.

have got

Positive

I You We They	have	got	a cat. a garden.
He She It	has		

Negative

I You We They	haven't	got	a dog. a garage.
He She It	hasn't		

Questions

Have	I you we they	got	any money? a sister?
Has	he she it		

How many children **have they got**?

Short answers
Yes, I have./No, I haven't.
Yes, she has./No, she hasn't.

have

Positive

I You We They	have		a cat. a garden.
He She It	has		

Negative

I You We They	don't	have	a dog. a garage.
He She It	doesn't		

Questions

Do	I you we they	have	any money? a sister?
Does	he she it		

How many children **do they have**?

Short answers
Yes, I do./No, I don't.
Yes, she does./No, she doesn't.

The past of both *have* and *have got* is *had*.

10.3 Prepositions

The country is quieter **than** the city.
The house is 50 metres **from** the sea.
Everest is the highest mountain **in** the world.
He spends his time **on** the banks of the river.
She came **out of** the garage.
He drove **along** the road.
They ran **over** the bridge.
I walked **past** the pub.
He walked **up** the hill.
He ran **down** the hill.
The boat went **across** the river.
The cat ran **through** the hedge.
He jumped **into** the lake.

Unit 11

11.1 Present Continuous

1   The Present Continuous describes an activity happening now.
    She**'s wearing** jeans.
    I**'m studying** English.

2   It also describes an activity in the near future.
    I**'m playing** tennis this afternoon.
    Jane**'s seeing** her boyfriend tonight.

Positive and Negative

I	am		
He She It	is	(not) going	outside.
We You They	are		

Question

	am	I	
Where	is	he/she/it	going?
	are	we you they	

Yes/No questions	Short answers
Are you having a good time?	Yes, we are.
Is my English getting better?	Yes, it is.
Are they having a party?	No, they aren't.

Spelling of verb + -ing

1   Most verbs just add -ing.
    wear   wea**ring**
    go   go**ing**
    cook   cook**ing**
    hold   hold**ing**

2   If the infinitive ends in -e, drop the -e.
    write   writ**ing**
    smile   smil**ing**
    take   tak**ing**

3   When a one-syllable verb has one vowel and ends in a consonant, double the consonant.
    sit   si**tt**ing
    get   ge**tt**ing
    run   ru**nn**ing

11.2 Present Simple and Present Continuous

1   The Present Simple describes things that are always true, or true for a long time.
    I **come** from Switzerland.
    He **works** in a bank.

2   The Present Continuous describes activities happening now, and temporary activities.
    Why **are you wearing** a suit? You usually wear jeans.

11.3 *Whose* + possessive pronouns

Whose … ? asks about possession.

Subject	Object	Adjective	Pronoun
I	me	my	mine
You	you	your	yours
He	him	his	his
She	her	her	hers
We	us	our	ours
They	them	their	theirs

Whose is this book? Whose book is this? Whose is it?	It's	mine. yours. hers. his. ours. theirs.

11.4 Prepositions

I read **in** bed.
We've got this jumper **in** red.
He's talking **to** Mandy.
There's a girl **with** fair hair.
I'm looking **for** a jumper.
I always pay **by** credit card.

Unit 12

12.1 *going to*

1   *Going to* expresses a person's plans and intentions.
      She's **going to** be a ballet dancer when she grows up.
      We're **going to** stay in a villa in France this summer.

2   Often there is no difference between *going to* and the Present Continuous to refer to a future intention.
      I**'m seeing** Peter tonight.
      I**'m going to see** Peter tonight.

3   We also use *going to* when we can see now that something is sure to happen in the future.
      Careful! That glass is **going to** fall!

Positive and negative

I	am		
He/She/It	is	(not) going to	have a break.
We You They	are		stay at home.

Question

	am	I		
	is	he/she/it	going to	have a break?
When	are	we you they		stay at home?

With the verbs *to go* and *to come*, we usually use the Present Continuous for future plans.
    We**'re going** to Paris next week.
    Joe and Tim **are coming** for lunch tomorrow.

12.2 Infinitive of purpose

The infinitive can express why a person does something.
    I'm saving my money **to buy** a CD player.
    (= because I want to buy a CD player)

    We're going to Paris **to have** a holiday.
    (= because we want to have a holiday)

    NOT
    I'm saving my money ~~for to buy~~ a CD player.
    I'm saving my money ~~for buy~~ a CD player.

12.3 Prepositions

I'm going to Florida **in** a year's time.
He's interested **in** flying.
She's good **at** singing.
She was afraid **of** cars.
What's the weather **like**?
What's **on** TV tonight?
There's a film **on** Channel 4.
What's **on at** the cinema?

Unit 13

13.1 Question forms

When did Columbus discover America?
Where are the Andes?
Who did she marry?
Who was Mother Teresa?
How do you get to school?
What do you have for breakfast?
What happens at the end of the story?
Why do you want to learn English?

How many people are there in the class?
How much does she earn?
How far is it to the centre?
What sort of car do you have?
Which newspaper do you read?

13.2 Adjectives and adverbs

Adjectives describe nouns.
    a **big** dog
    a **careful** driver

Adverbs describe verbs.
    She ran **quickly**.
    He drives too **fast**.

To form regular adverbs, add *-ly* to the adjective.
Words ending in *-y* change to *-ily*.

Adjective	Adverb
quick	quickly
bad	badly
careful	carefully
immediate	immediately
easy	easily

Some adverbs are irregular.

Adjective	Adverb
good	well
hard	hard
early	early
fast	fast

13.3 Prepositions

What's the story **about**?
What happens **at** the end of the story?
The train leaves **from** platform 9.

Unit 14

14.1 Present Perfect

1   The Present Perfect refers to an action that happened some time before now.
    She's **travelled** to most parts of the world.
    Have you ever **been** in a car accident?

2   If we want to say *when* these actions happened, we must use the Past Simple.
    She **went** to Russia two years ago.
    I **was** in a crash when I was 10.

3   Notice the time expressions used with the Past Simple.

I left	last night. yesterday. in 1990. at three o'clock. on Monday.

Positive and negative

I You We They	have	(not) been	to the States.
He She It	has		

I've been = I have been
You've been = You have been
We've been = We have been
They've been = They have been

He's been = He has been
She's been = She has been
It's been = It has been

Question

Where	have	I you we they	been?
	has	she he it	

Yes/No **questions**
Have you been to Russia?

Short answers
Yes, I have.
No, I haven't.

ever and *never*

We use *ever* in questions and *never* in negative sentences.
    Have you **ever** been to Russia?
    I've **never** been to Russia.

14.2 *yet* and *just*

We use *just* in positive sentences. We use *yet* in negative sentences and questions.
    Have you done your homework **yet**?
    I haven't done it **yet** (but I'm going to).
    I have **just** done it (a short time before now).

14.3 *been* and *gone*

She's **gone** to Portugal (and she's there now).
She's **been** to Portugal (sometime in her life, but now she has returned).

14.4 Prepositions

She works **for** a big company.
Hamlet is a play **by** Shakespeare.
Brad and Marilyn are **on** honeymoon
Wait **for** me!

Word list

Here is a list of most of the new words in the units of New Headway Elementary.

adj = adjective
adv = adverb
conj = conjunction
opp = opposite
pl = plural
prep = preposition
pron = pronoun
pp = past participle
n = noun
v = verb
infml = informal
US = American English

Unit 1

apple *n* /'æpl/
bag *n* /bæg/
because *conj* /bɪ'kɒz/
Brazil *n* /brə'zɪl/
brother *n* /'brʌðə/
camera *n* /'kæmərə/
children *n pl* /'tʃɪldrən/
cinema *n* /'sɪnəmə/
country *n* /'kʌntri/
day *n* /deɪ/
dictionary *n* /'dɪkʃənri/
doctor *n* /'dɒktə/
Egypt *n* /'iːdʒɪpt/
England *n* /'ɪŋglənd/
evening *n* /'iːvnɪŋ/
extension *n* /ɪk'stenʃən/
fine *adj* /faɪn/
flat *n* /flæt/
France *n* /frɑːns/
from *prep* /frɒm/
Germany *n* /'dʒɜːməni/
goodbye /gʊd'baɪ/
have *v* /hæv/
hello /hə'ləʊ/
her *pron* /hɜː/
house *n* /haʊs/
Hungary *n* /'hʌŋgəri/
international *adj* /ˌɪntə'næʃnəl/
Italy *n* /'ɪtəli/
Japan *n* /dʒə'pæn/
job *n* /dʒɒb/
key *n* /kiː/
language *n* /'læŋgwɪdʒ/
learn *v* /lɜːn/
letter *n* /'letə/
live *v* /lɪv/
magazine *n* /mægə'ziːn/
married *adj* /'mærɪd/
me *pron* /miː/
Mexico *n* /'meksɪkəʊ/
my *pron* /maɪ/
name *n* /neɪm/
newspaper *n* /'njuːspeɪpə/
nice *adj* /naɪs/
not bad *adj infml* /ˌnɒt 'bæd/
orange *n* /'ɒrɪndʒ/
postcard *n* /'pəʊskɑːd/
Russia *n* /'rʌʃə/
see you *v infml* /'siː juː/
sister *n* /'sɪstə/
Spain *n* /speɪn/
stamp *n* /stæmp/
student *n* /'stjuːdənt/
teacher *n* /'tiːtʃə/
telephone number *n* /'teləfəʊn ˌnʌmbə/
thank you /'θæŋk juː/
thanks /θæŋks/
the USA *n* /ðə ˌjuːes'eɪ/
this (book) /ðɪs/
ticket *n* /'tɪkɪt/
want *v* /wɒnt/
where *adv* /weə/
your *pron* /jɔː/

Unit 2

accountant *n* /ə'kaʊntənt/
address *n* /ə'dres/
age *n* /eɪdʒ/
American *adj* /ə'merɪkən/
anything else /'eniθɪŋ 'els/
apartment *n* /ə'pɑːtmənt/
Argentina *n* /ˌɑːdʒən'tiːnə/
at home /ət 'həʊm/
aunt *n* /ɑːnt/
big *adj* /bɪg/
boyfriend *n* /'bɔɪfrend/
brother *n* /'brʌðə/
cake *n* /keɪk/
Can I have … ? /ˌkæn aɪ 'hæv/
Can I help? /ˌkæn aɪ 'help/
cheap *adj* /tʃiːp/
chicken *n* /'tʃɪkɪn/
chips *n pl* /tʃɪps/
chocolate *n* /'tʃɒklət/
coffee *n* /'kɒfi/
coffee bar *n* /'kɒfi ˌbɑː/
cold *adj* /kəʊld/
college *n* /'kɒlɪdʒ/
dancer *n* /'dɑːnsə/
daughter *n* /'dɔːtə/
different *adj* /'dɪfrənt/
difficult *adj* /'dɪfɪkəlt/
drink *v* /drɪŋk/
easy *adj* /'iːzi/
egg *n* /eg/
exciting *adj* /ɪk'saɪtɪŋ/
expensive *adj* /ɪk'spensɪv/
fast *adj* /fɑːst/
father *n* /'fɑːðə/
first name *n* /'fɜːst neɪm/
French *adj* /frentʃ/
friendly *adj* /'frendli/
girl *n* /gɜːl/
girlfriend *n* /'gɜːlfrend/
good *adj* /gʊd/
grandfather *n* /'grænfɑːðə/
grandmother *n* /'grænmʌðə/

hamburger *n* /'hæmbɜːgə/
happy *adj* /'hæpi/
here *adv* /hɪə/
here you are /'hɪə juː ˌɑː/
hi /haɪ/
holiday *n* /'hɒlɪdeɪ/
horrible *adj* /'hɒrəbl/
hot *adj* /hɒt/
how much? *adv* /ˌhaʊ 'mʌtʃ/
how old? *adv* /ˌhaʊ 'əʊld/
husband *n* /'hʌzbənd/
ice-cream *n* /'aɪskriːm/
identity card *n* /aɪ'dentɪti ˌkɑːd/
Ireland *n* /'aɪələnd/
journalist *n* /'dʒɜːnəlɪst/
love *n* /lʌv/
lovely *adj* /'lʌvli/
menu *n* /'menjuː/
mineral water *n* /'mɪnərəl ˌwɔːtə/
morning *n* /'mɔːnɪŋ/
mother *n* /'mʌðə/
new *adj* /njuː/
now *adv* /naʊ/
nurse *n* /nɜːs/
old *adj* /əʊld/
orange juice *n* /'ɒrɪndʒ ˌdʒuːs/
pardon? /'pɑːdn/
photo *n* /'fəʊtəʊ/
pizza *n* /'piːtsə/
please /pliːz/
Poland *n* /'pəʊlənd/
policeman *n* /pə'liːsmən/
pound *n* /paʊnd/
practice *n* /'præktɪs/
price *n* /praɪs/
salad *n* /'sæləd/
slow *adj* /sləʊ/
small *adj* /smɔːl/
snack bar *n* /'snæk ˌbɑː/
snow *n, v* /snəʊ/
son *n* /sʌn/
soon *adv* /suːn/
speak *v* /spiːk/
subway *n US* /'sʌbweɪ/
surname *n* /'sɜːneɪm/
Switzerland *n* /'swɪtsələnd/
tea *n* /tiː/
tuna *n* /'tjuːnə/
uncle *n* /'ʌnkl/
understand *v* /ʌndə'stænd/
use *v* /juːz/
who? *pron* /huː/
wife *n* /waɪf/
write *v* /raɪt/
young *adj* /jʌŋ/

Unit 3

a little *adj* /ə 'lɪtl/
afternoon *n* /ˌɑːftə'nuːn/
ambulance *n* /'æmbjuːləns/
architect *n* /'ɑːkɪtekt/
Australia *n* /ɒ'streɪlɪə/
barman *n* /'bɑːmən/
be quiet *v* /ˌbiː 'kwaɪət/
beer *n* /bɪə/
before *prep* /bɪ'fɔː/
biology *n* /baɪ'ɒlədʒi/
boat *n* /bəʊt/
breakfast *n* /'brekfəst/
busy *adj* /'bɪzi/
but *conj* /bʌt/, /bət/
centre *n* /'sentə/
city *n* /'sɪti/
clock *n* /klɒk/
collect *v* /kə'lekt/
come *v* /kʌm/
day *n* /deɪ/
deliver *v* /dɪ'lɪvə/
design *v* /dɪ'zaɪn/
do the accounts *v*
    /ˌduː ði ə'kaʊnts/
dog *n* /dɒg/
drive *n* /draɪv/
end *n* /end/
every day *adv* /ˌevri 'deɪ/
Excuse me /ɪk'skjuːz 'miː/
fireman *n* /'faɪəmən/
fly *v* /flaɪ/
flying doctor *n* /ˌflaɪɪŋ 'dɒktə/
football *n* /'fʊtbɔːl/
free time *n* /ˌfriː 'taɪm/
German *adj* /'dʒɜːmən/
get up *v* /ˌget 'ʌp/
glass *n* /glɑːs/
go *v* /gəʊ/
go to bed *v* /ˌgəʊ tə 'bed/
guest *n* /gest/
help *v* /help/
hospital *n* /'hɒspɪtl/
house *n* /haʊs/
How's (Ann)? *adv* /haʊz/
hurry up *v* /ˌhʌri 'ʌp/
interpreter *n* /ɪn'tɜːprɪtə/
island *n* /'aɪlənd/
language *n* /'læŋgwɪdʒ/
late *adj* /leɪt/
like *v* /laɪk/
listen *v* /'lɪsən/
look after *v* /ˌlʊk 'ɑːftə/
love *v* /lʌv/
make *v* /meɪk/
man *n* /mæn/
money *n* /'mʌni/
music *n* /'mjuːzɪk/
never *adv* /'nevə/
non-stop *adv* /ˌnɒn 'stɒp/
north *n* /nɔːθ/
office *n* /'ɒfɪs/
only *adj* /'əʊnli/
ordinary *adj* /'ɔːdənri/

people *n pl* /'piːpl/
perhaps *adv* /pə'hæps/
petrol *n* /'petrəl/
pilot *n* /'paɪlət/
plane *n* /pleɪn/
play *v* /pleɪ/
post *n* /pəʊst/
postman *n* /'pəʊsmən/
pub *n* /pʌb/
radio *n* /'reɪdɪəʊ/
school *n* /skuːl/
scientist *n* /'saɪəntɪst/
sell *v* /sel/
serve *v* /sɜːv/
shop *n* /ʃɒp/
shopkeeper *n* /'ʃɒpkiːpə/
sick *adj* /sɪk/
sit down *v* /ˌsɪt 'daʊn/
skiing *n* /'skiːɪŋ/
small *adj* /smɔːl/
speak *v* /spiːk/
summer *n* /'sʌmə/
supper *n* /'sʌpə/
taxi driver *n* /'tæksi ˌdraɪvə/
television *n* /'telɪvɪʒn/
tennis *n* /'tenɪs/
that's right /ˌðæts 'raɪt/
there *adv* /ðeə/
thing *n* /θɪŋ/
tired *adj* /'taɪəd/
too *adv* /tuː/
tourist *n* /'tʊərɪst/
town *n* /taʊn/
translate *v* /trænz'leɪt/
undertaker *n* /'ʌndəteɪkə/
vanilla *adj* /və'nɪlə/
walk *n, v* /wɔːk/
watch *n, v* /wɒtʃ/
week *n* /wiːk/
weekday *n* /'wiːkdeɪ/
wine *n* /waɪn/
winter *n* /'wɪntə/
work *v* /wɜːk/
world *n* /wɜːld/

Unit 4

a lot *pron* /ə 'lɒt/
after *adv* /'ɑːftə/
always *adv* /'ɔːlweɪz/
Autumn *n* /'ɔːtəm/
bad *adj* /bæd/
bar *n* /bɑː/
baseball *n* /'beɪsbɔːl/
beach *n* /biːtʃ/
block *n* /blɒk/
boring *adj* /'bɔːrɪŋ/
brown *adj* /braʊn/
bus *n* /bʌs/
buy *v* /baɪ/
called *pp* /kɔːld/
car *n* /kɑː/
chat *v* /tʃæt/
Chinese *adj* /tʃaɪ'niːz/
colour *n* /'kʌlə/
come *v* /kʌm/
computer *n* /kəm'pjuːtə/
computer game *n*
    /kəm'pjuːtə geɪm/
cook *v* /kʊk/
dance *v* /dɑːns/
different *adj* /'dɪfrənt/
dinner *n* /'dɪnə/
do *v* /duː/
domestic *adj* /də'mestɪk/
don't worry *v* /ˌdəʊnt 'wʌri/
early *adj* /'ɜːli/
especially *adv* /ɪ'speʃəli/
every day *adv* /ˌevri 'deɪ/
Excuse me /ɪk'skjuːz 'miː/
export department *n*
    /'ekspɔːt dɪˌpɑːtmənt/
exposure *n* /ɪk'spəʊʒə/
fall (= autumn) *n US* /fɔːl/
family *n* /'fæməli/
famous *adj* /'feɪməs/
fantastic *adj* /fæn'tæstɪk/
favourite *adj* /'feɪvrɪt/
film *n* /fɪlm/
flower *n* /'flaʊə/
food *n* /fuːd/
fortunately *adv* /'fɔːtʃənətli/
friend *n* /frend/
go out *v* /ˌgəʊ 'aʊt/
gold *adj* /gəʊld/
grey *adj* /greɪ/
gym *n* /dʒɪm/
headquarters *n pl* /ˌhed'kwɔːtəz/
here *adv* /hɪə/
hobby *n* /'hɒbi/
hour *n* /aʊə/
how? *adv* /haʊ/
I'm sorry /ˌaɪm 'sɒri/
ice hockey *n* /'aɪs ˌhɒki/
ice-skating *n* /'aɪs ˌskeɪtɪŋ/
interesting *adj* /'ɪntrəstɪŋ/
interview *n* /'ɪntəvjuː/
it doesn't matter /ɪt 'dʌznt 'mætə/
jogging *n* /'dʒɒgɪŋ/
kid *n* /kɪd/

lake *n* /leɪk/
learn *v* /lɜːn/
leisure activity *n*
    /'leʒə(r) æk'tɪvəti/
long *adj* /lɒŋ/
make *v* /meɪk/
meet *v* /miːt/
near *adv* /nɪə/
never *adv* /'nevə/
news programme *n*
    /'njuːz ˌprəʊgræm/
next *adj* /nekst/
of course /əv 'kɔːs/
often *adv* /'ɒfən/, /'ɒftən/
only *adj* /'əʊnli/
open *v* /'əʊpən/
pardon? /pɑːdn/
parents *n pl* /'peərənts/
pop song *n* /'pɒp sɒŋ/
Portugal *n* /'pɔːtʃʊgl/
reading *n* /'riːdɪŋ/
really? /'rɪəli/
red *adj* /red/
relax *v* /rɪ'læks/
sailing *n* /'seɪlɪŋ/
say *v* /seɪ/
season *n* /'siːzn/
short *adj* /ʃɔːt/
shy *adj* /ʃaɪ/
smoke *v* /sməʊk/
sometimes *adv* /'sʌmtaɪmz/
special *adj* /'speʃl/
Spring *n* /sprɪŋ/
start *v* /stɑːt/
suddenly *adv* /'sʌdnli/
sunbathing *n* /'sʌnbeɪθɪŋ/
sunny *adj* /'sʌni/
swimming *n* /'swɪmɪŋ/
take *v* /teɪk/
take photos *v* /'teɪk 'fəʊtəz/
That's OK /'ðæts əʊˌkeɪ/
then *adv* /ðen/
traffic *n* /'træfɪk/
tree *n* /triː/
usually *adj* /'juːʒəli/
visit *v* /'vɪzɪt/
warm *adj* /wɔːm/
weekend *n* /'wiːkend/
wet *adj* /wet/
What does ... mean?
    /wɒt dʌz ... miːn/
what time? /wɒt 'taɪm/
what? /wɒt/
when? /wen/
where? /weə/
why? /waɪ/
window *n* /'wɪndəʊ/
year *n* /jɪə/
yellow *adj* /'jeləʊ/

Unit 5

address book n /ə'dres ˌbʊk/
air conditioning n
　　/'eə kənˌdɪʃnɪŋ/
alone adj /ə'ləʊn/
armchair n /'ɑ:mtʃeə/
at the moment adv
　　/ˌæt ðə 'məʊmənt/
bank n /bæŋk/
bathroom n /'bɑ:θrʊm/
beautiful adj /'bju:tɪfl/
bedroom n /'bedrʊm/
best adj /best/
blinds n pl /blaɪndz/
bookshelf n /'bʊkʃelf/
both /bəʊθ/
briefcase n /'bri:fkeɪs/
bus ticket n /'bʌs ˌtɪkɪt/
cat n /kæt/
CD n /ˌsi: 'di:/
champagne n /ʃæm'peɪn/
Cheers! /tʃɪəz/
chemist('s) n /'kemɪst(s)/
clock n /klɒk/
cockpit n /'kɒkpɪt/
coffee table n /'kɒfi ˌteɪbl/
comfortable adj /'kʌmftəbl/
cooker n /'kʊkə/
cup n /kʌp/
cupboard n /'kʌbəd/
dishwasher n /'dɪʃwɒʃə/
door n /dɔ:/
downstairs adv /ˌdaʊn'steəz/
emergency exit n
　　/ɪ'mɜ:dʒənsi ˌeksɪt/
everything pron /'evriθɪŋ/
exactly adv /ɪg'zæktli/
ex-wife n /ˌeks'waɪf/
famous adj /'feɪməs/
fantastic adj /fæn'tæstɪk/
far adv /fɑ:/
film star n /'fɪlm ˌstɑ:/
fire n /faɪə/
first /fɜ:st/
first class adj /'fɜ:st 'klɑ:s/
flat n /flæt/
flight attendant n
　　/'flaɪt əˌtendənt/
floor n /flɔ:/
fork n /fɔ:k/
fridge n /frɪdʒ/
front door n /ˌfrʌnt 'dɔ:/
garden n /'gɑ:dn/
grandma n /'grænmɑ:/
how many? /ˌhaʊ 'meni/
just (= only) adv /dʒʌst/
key n /ki:/
kitchen n /'kɪtʃɪn/
knife n /naɪf/
lady n /'leɪdi/
lamp n /læmp/
left adv (opp right) /left/
living room n /'lɪvɪŋ ˌrʊm/
lots (of books) /lɒts/
luxury n /'lʌkʃəri/

mirror n /'mɪrə/
mobile phone n /'məʊbaɪl 'fəʊn/
modern adj /'mɒdn/
most of the time
　　/'məʊst əv ðə ˌtaɪm/
neighbour n /'neɪbə/
newsagent('s) n /'nju:zeɪdʒənt(s)/
notebook n /'nəʊtbʊk/
open v /'əʊpən/
over there /ˌəʊvə 'ðeə/
park n /pɑ:k/
party n /'pɑ:ti/
passport n /'pɑ:spɔ:t/
pen n /pen/
picture n /'pɪktʃə/
plane n /pleɪn/
plant n /plɑ:nt/
plate n /pleɪt/
quite (big) adv /kwaɪt/
rain v /reɪn/
rich adj /rɪtʃ/
right adv (opp left) /raɪt/
room n /rʊm/, /ru:m/
rug n /rʌg/
sandwich n /'sænwɪdʒ/
second /'sekənd/
section n /'sekʃn/
shelf n /ʃelf/
shop n /ʃɒp/
sofa n /'səʊfə/
spoon n /spu:n/
stop (bus) n /stɒp/
steps n /steps/
stereo n /'steriəʊ/
supermarket n /'su:pəˌmɑ:kɪt/
swimming pool n /'swɪmɪŋ ˌpu:l/
thanks a lot /'θæŋks ə ˌlɒt/
toilet n /'tɔɪlət/
top n /tɒp/
upstairs adv /ˌʌp'steəz/
wall n /wɔ:l/
washing machine n
　　/'wɒʃɪŋ məˌʃi:n/

Unit 6

bedtime n /'bedtaɪm/
between prep /bɪ'twi:n/
bike n /baɪk/
brilliant adj /'brɪliənt/
can't stop v /'kɑ:nt 'stɒp/
Canada n /'kænədə/
check v /tʃek/
chess n /tʃes/
concert n /'kɒnsət/
conversation n /kɒnvə'seɪʃn/
do homework v /ˌdu: 'həʊmwɜ:k/
eye n /aɪ/
fall in love v /ˌfɔ:l ɪn 'lʌv/
family n /'fæməli/
feel v /fi:l/
football n /'fʊtbɔ:l/
genius n /'dʒi:niəs/
hear v /hɪə/
her pron /hɜ:/
his pron /hɪz/
hour n /aʊə/
house n /haʊs/
initial n /ɪ'nɪʃl/
Italian adj /ɪ'tæliən/
Japanese adj /dʒæpə'ni:z/
know v /nəʊ/
large adj /lɑ:dʒ/
last month adv /ˌlɑ:st 'mʌnθ/
laugh v /lɑ:f/
little adj /'lɪtl/
manager n /'mænɪdʒə/
message n /'mesɪdʒ/
now adv /naʊ/
our pron /aʊə/
paint v /peɪnt/
pianist n /'pɪənɪst/
piano n /pi'ænəʊ/
poetry n /'pəʊətri/
Portuguese adj /ˌpɔ:tʃʊ'gi:z/
poor adj /pɔ:/
practise v /'præktɪs/
question n /'kwestʃən/
really adv /'ri:əli/
require v /rɪ'kwaɪə/
sad adj /sæd/
save v /seɪv/
sea n /si:/
see v /si:/
sell v /sel/
Spanish adj /'spænɪʃ/
spell v /spel/
spelling n /'spelɪŋ/
spend v /spend/
style n /staɪl/
sun n /sʌn/
swim v /swɪm/
their pron /ðeə/
think v /θɪŋk/
today adv /tə'deɪ/
travel v /'trævl/

until conj /ʌn'tɪl/
use v /ju:z/
very adv /'veri/
very well adv /ˌveri 'wel/
was born v /wəz 'bɔ:n/
wear v /weə/
wedding n /'wedɪŋ/
well adv /wel/
yesterday adv /'jestədeɪ/
yesterday evening adv
　　/ˌjestədeɪ 'i:vnɪŋ/

Unit 7

advertising agency *n*
  /'ædvətaɪzɪŋ ˌeɪdʒənsi/
afraid *adj* /ə'freɪd/
after that *adv* /ˌɑ:ftə 'ðæt/
agree *v* /ə'gri:/
army *n* /'ɑ:mi/
at night *adv* /ət 'naɪt/
bath *n* /bɑ:θ/
become *v* /bɪ'kʌm/
begin *v* /bɪ'gɪn/
birthday *n* /'bɜ:θdeɪ/
bomb *v* /bɒm/
build *v* /bɪld/
businessman *n* /'bɪznɪsmæn/
buy *v* /baɪ/

capital *adj* /'kæpɪtl/
car crash *n* /'kɑ:ˌkræʃ/
century *n* /'sentʃəri/
chemistry *n* /'kemɪstri/
child *n* /tʃaɪld/
Christmas *n* /'krɪsməs/
congratulations
  /kənˌgrætʃʊ'leɪʃnz/
cotton field *n* /'kɒtn ˌfi:ld/
create *v* /kri'eɪt/

die *v* /daɪ/
dinner *n* /'dɪnə/

earn *v* /ɜ:n/
Easter Day *n* /'i:stə ˌdeɪ/
education *n* /edʒʊ'keɪʃn/
end *v* /end/
Euro *n* /'jʊərəʊ/
event *n* /ɪ'vent/
everybody *pron* /'evrɪbɒdi/

farm *n* /fɑ:m/
farmer *n* /'fɑ:mə/
fight *v* /faɪt/
finally *adv* /'faɪnəli/
first (... next) *adv* /fɜ:st/
funeral *n* /'fju:nərəl/

great grandparents *n pl*
  /ˌgreɪt 'grænpeərənts/
grocer *n* /'grəʊsə/
grow *v* /grəʊ/

Hallowe'en *n* /ˌhæləʊ'i:n/
happen *v* /'hæpn/
hate *v* /heɪt/
have a holiday *v* /ˌhæv ə 'hɒlədeɪ/
horse *n* /hɔ:s/

immediately *adv* /ɪ'mi:dɪətli/
important *adj* /ɪm'pɔ:tənt/
independence *n* /ɪndɪ'pendəns/
iron *adj* /'aɪən/

kiss *v* /kɪs/

later *adv* /'leɪtə/
leader *n* /'li:də/
leave *v* /li:v/
life *n* /laɪf/
listen *v* /'lɪsn/
little (money) /'lɪtl/
look *v* /lʊk/
lose *v* /lu:z/
lucky *adj* /'lʌki/

marry *v* /'mæri/
midnight *n* /'mɪdnaɪt/
million /'mɪljən/
moon *n* /mu:n/
Mother's Day *n* /'mʌðəz ˌdeɪ/

need *v* /ni:d/
New Year's Eve /ˌnju: jɪəz 'i:v/
nineties *n pl* /'naɪntiz/

own *v* /əʊn/

pardon? /'pɑ:dn/
personality *n* /ˌpɜ:sə'næləti/
poem *n* /'pəʊɪm/
politician *n* /ˌpɒlə'tɪʃn/
politics *n* /'pɒlətɪks/
present (= birthday) *n* /'preznt/
president *n* /'prezɪdənt/
prime minister *n*
  /ˌpraɪm 'mɪnɪstə/
problem *n* /'prɒbləm/

read *v* /ri:d/
remember *v* /rɪ'membə/
resign *v* /'rɪzaɪn/

same to you /'seɪm tə 'ju:/
sit *v* /sɪt/
slave *n* /sleɪv/
sleep *v* /sli:p/
soldier *n* /'səʊldʒə/
soon *adv* /su:n/
start *v* /stɑ:t/
strong *adj* /strɒŋ/
study *v* /'stʌdi/
subject (school) *n* /'sʌbdʒekt/
sure *adj* /ʃʊə/, /ʃɔ:/
survive *v* /sə'vaɪv/

tear (+ cry) *n* /tɪə/
terrorist *n* /'terərɪst/
thank goodness /'θæŋk 'gʊdnes/
Thanksgiving *n* /θæŋks'gɪvɪŋ/
theatre *n* /'θɪətə/
think *v* /θɪŋk/
tobacco *n* /tə'bækəʊ/
together *adv* /tə'geðə/
tomorrow *adv* /tə'mɒrəʊ/
twin *n* /twɪn/
university *n* /ju:nɪ'vɜ:səti/
Valentine's Day *n*
  /'væləntaɪnz ˌdeɪ/
video *n* /'vɪdɪəʊ/

war *n* /wɔ:/
wedding day *n* /'wedɪŋ ˌdeɪ/
widow *n* /'wɪdəʊ/
win *v* /wɪn/
work hard *v* /'wɜ:k 'hɑ:d/
wrong *adj* /rɒŋ/

Unit 8

(3 years) ago *adv* /ə'gəʊ/
(coffee) break *n* /breɪk/
arthritis *n* /ɑ:'θraɪtɪs/
aspirin *n* /'æsprɪn/
astronaut *n* /'æstrənɔ:t/

banana *n* /bə'nɑ:nə/
beach *n* /bi:tʃ/
bestselling *adj* /'best'selɪŋ/
blue *adj* /blu:/
bottle *n* /'bɒtl/
boy *n* /bɔɪ/

chat *v* /tʃæt/
chatline *n* /'tʃætlaɪn/
chicken *n* /'tʃɪkɪn/
clock *n* /klɒk/
cloth *n* /klɒθ/
company *n* /'kʌmpəni/
couple *n pl* /'kʌpl/

date *n* /deɪt/
delicious *adj* /dɪ'lɪʃəs/
drug *n* /drʌg/

e-mail *n* /'i:meɪl/
exam *n* /ɪg'zæm/

face *n* /feɪs/
face to face /'feɪs tə 'feɪs/
fashionable *adj* /'fæʃnəbl/
fax *n* /fæks/
fisherman *n* /'fɪʃəmən/
funny *adj* /'fʌni/

get engaged *v* /ˌget ɪn'geɪdʒd/
get married *v* /ˌget 'mærid/
go to a party *v* /ˌgəʊ tu: ə 'pɑ:ti/
good luck! /ˌgʊd 'lʌk/
green *adj* /gri:n/

in a hurry /ˌɪn ə 'hʌri/
incredible *adj* /ɪn'kredəbl/
internet *n* /'ɪntənet/
invention *n* /ɪn'venʃn/

jeans *n pl* /dʒi:nz/
joke *n* /dʒəʊk/

leg *n* /leg/

mobile phone *n* /'məʊbaɪl 'fəʊn/
moon *n* /mu:n/
mouth *n* /maʊθ/

nervous *adj* /'nɜ:vəs/
nowadays *adv* /'naʊədeɪz/

painkiller *n* /'peɪnkɪlə/
philosopher *n* /fɪ'losəfə/
phone call *n* /'fəʊn ˌkɔ:l/
produce *v* /prə'dju:s/
public holiday *n*
  /'pʌblɪk 'hɒlədeɪ/

recipe *n* /'resəpi/
record (for music) *n* /'rekɔ:d/
ride *v* /raɪd/
rose *n* /rəʊz/

send *v* /send/

take *v* /teɪk/
term *n* /tɜ:m/
them *pron* /ðem/
throw *v* /θrəʊ/
transmit *v* /trænz'mɪt/
trousers *n pl* /'traʊzəz/
true *adj* /tru:/
true love *n* /ˌtru: 'lʌv/

vacuum cleaner *n*
  /'vækju:m ˌkli:nə/
watch *v* /wɒtʃ/
way *n* /weɪ/
women *n pl* /'wɪmɪn/
workmen *n pl*
  /'wɜ:kmen/, /'wɜ:kmən/
workroom *n* /'wɜ:krʊm/
worried *adj* /'wʌrid/

Unit 9

a bit *n* /ə ˈbɪt/
all sorts *n pl* /ˈɔːl ˈsɔːts/
anybody *pron* /ˈenibɒdi/
anyway *adv* /ˈeniweɪ/
apple juice *n* /ˈæpl ˌdʒuːs/
away from *adv* /əˈweɪ frəm/
bacon *n* /ˈbeɪkən/
bag *n* /bæg/
bar of chocolate *n*
   /ˈbɑː(r) əv ˈtʃɒklət/
beer *n* /bɪə/
birthday *n* /ˈbɜːθdeɪ/
biscuit *n* /ˈbɪskɪt/
black (coffee) *adj* /blæk/
borrow *v* /ˈbɒrəʊ/
bottle *n* /ˈbɒtl/
bread *n* /bred/
carrot *n* /ˈkærət/
central *adj* /ˈsentrəl/
cheese *n* /tʃiːz/
China *n* /ˈtʃaɪnə/
Chinese *adj* /tʃaɪˈniːz/
chopsticks *n pl* /ˈtʃɒpstɪks/
cigarette *n* /sɪgəˈret/
control *v* /kənˈtrəʊl/
course (of a meal) *n* /kɔːs/
curry *n* /ˈkʌri/
dangerous *adj* /ˈdeɪndʒərəs/
depend *v* /dɪˈpend/
dessert *n* /dɪˈzɜːt/
disgusting *adj* /dɪsˈgʌstɪŋ/
easily *adv* /ˈiːzəli/
egg *n* /eg/
either *adv* /ˈaɪðə/
environment *n* /ɪnˈvaɪrənmənt/
especially /ɪˈspeʃəli/
farm *v* /fɑːm/
finger *n* /ˈfɪŋgə/
fish *n* /fɪʃ/
fizzy water *n* /ˈfɪzi ˈwɔːtə/
for example /ˌfɔː(r) ɪgˈzɑːmpl/
foreign *adj* /ˈfɒrɪn/
fruit *n* /fruːt/
full *adj* /fʊl/
glad *adj* /glæd/
ham *n* /hæm/
herring *n* /ˈherɪŋ/
history *n* /ˈhɪstəri/
horrible *adj* /ˈhɒrəbl/
human *adj* /ˈhjuːmən/
hungry *adj* /ˈhʌŋgri/
land *n* /lænd/
main (meal) *adj* /meɪn/
meal *n* /miːl/
meat *n* /miːt/
milk *n* /mɪlk/
money *n* /ˈmʌni/
mushroom *n* /ˈmʌʃrʊm/
noodles *n pl* /ˈnuːdlz/
north *n* /nɔːθ/

part (of the world) *n* /pɑːt/
pass (= give) *v* /pɑːs/
pasta *n* /ˈpæstə/
pea *n* /piː/
petrol *n* /ˈpetrəl/
pick up *v* /ˌpɪk ˈʌp/
pocket *n* /ˈpɒkɪt/
poor *adj* /pʊə/, /pɔː/
possible *adj* /ˈpɒsəbl/
potatoes *n pl* /pəˈteɪtəʊz/
rice *n* /raɪs/
right now *adv* /ˌraɪt ˈnaʊ/
salt *n* /sɔːlt/, /sɒlt/
sardine *n* /sɑːˈdiːn/
sauce *n* /sɔːs/
sausages *n pl* /ˈsɒsɪdʒɪz/
shopping list *n* /ˈʃɒpɪŋ ˌlɪst/
south *n* /saʊθ/
still water *n* /ˈstɪl ˈwɔːtə/
strawberry *n* /ˈstrɔːbəri/
sugar *n* /ˈʃʊgə/
table *n* /ˈteɪbl/
terrible *adj* /ˈterəbl/
toast *n* /təʊst/
together *adv* /təˈgeðə/
tomato *n* /təˈmɑːtəʊ/
transport *v* /trænˈspɔːt/
typical *adj* /ˈtɪpɪkl/
vegetable *n* /ˈvedʒtəbl/
washing-up *n* /ˌwɒʃɪŋ ˈʌp/
wonderful *adj* /ˈwʌndəfʊl/
yoghurt *n* /ˈjɒgət/

Unit 10

art *n* /ɑːt/
blues (music) *n pl* /bluːz/
bridge *n* /brɪdʒ/
building *n* /ˈbɪldɪŋ/
busy *adj* /ˈbɪzi/
car park *n* /ˈkɑː ˌpɑːk/
carnival *n* /ˈkɑːnɪvl/
castle *n* /ˈkɑːsl/
cathedral *n* /kəˈθiːdrəl/
church *n* /tʃɜːtʃ/
clean *adj* /kliːn/
cosmopolitan *adj*
   /ˌkɒzməˈpɒlɪtən/
cottage *n* /ˈkɒtɪdʒ/
country (not the city) *n* /ˈkʌntri/
cousin *n* /ˈkʌzən/
cultural centre *n*
   /ˈkʌltʃərəl ˌsentə/
dangerous *adj* /ˈdeɪndʒərəs/
dirty *adj* /ˈdɜːti/
empire *n* /ˈempaɪə/
expensive *adj* /ɪkˈspensɪv/
factory *n* /ˈfæktri/
field *n* /fiːld/
found (a university) *v* /faʊnd/
garage *n* /ˈgærɪdʒ, ˈgærɑːʒ/
garden *n* /ˈgɑːdn/
gateway *n* /ˈgeɪtweɪ/
group *n* /gruːp/
hedge *n* /hedʒ/
hill *n* /hɪl/
hotel *n* /həʊˈtel/
hymn *n* /hɪm/
immigrants *n pl* /ˈɪmɪgrənts/
intelligent *adj* /ɪnˈtelɪdʒənt/
library *n* /ˈlaɪbrəri/
mixture *n* /ˈmɪkstʃə/
mountain *n* /ˈmaʊntɪn/
museum *n* /mjuːˈzɪəm/
night club *n* /ˈnaɪt ˌklʌb/
noisy *adj* /ˈnɔɪzi/
orchestra *n* /ˈɔːkɪstrə/
passenger *n* /ˈpæsɪndʒə/
popular *adj* /ˈpɒpjʊlə/
port *n* /pɔːt/
pretty *adj* /ˈprɪti/
quiet *adj* /ˈkwaɪət/
restaurant *n* /ˈrestrɒnt/
river bank *n* /ˈrɪvə ˌbæŋk/
rock group *n* /ˈrɒk ˌgruːp/
safe *adj* /seɪf/
ship *n* /ʃɪp/
small *adj* /smɔːl/
song *n* /sɒŋ/
spices *n pl* /ˈspaɪsɪz/
stand *v* /stænd/
street *n* /striːt/
tall *adj* /tɔːl/

the Underground *n*
   /ði ˈʌndəgraʊnd/
top ten (music) *adj* /ˌtɒp ˈten/
travel *n* /ˈtrævl/
unfriendly *adj* /ʌnˈfrendli/
village *n* /ˈvɪlɪdʒ/
wood *n* /wʊd/

Unit 11

baby *n* /'beɪbi/
baseball cap *n* /'beɪsbɔːl ˌkæp/
beautiful *adj* /'bjuːtɪfl/
bloom *v* /bluːm/
boot *n* /buːt/
bright *adj* /braɪt/
changing rooms *n pl*
    /'tʃeɪndʒɪŋ ˌruːmz/
chewing gum *n* /'tʃuːɪŋ ˌgʌm/
choose *v* /tʃuːz/
cigar *n* /sɪ'gɑː/
cloud *n* /klaʊd/
coat *n* /kəʊt/
credit card *n* /'kredɪt ˌkɑːd/
cry *v* /kraɪ/
dark *adj* /dɑːk/
dress *n* /dres/
eat *v* /iːt/
fair (hair) *adj* /feə/
fresh adj /freʃ/
good-looking *adj* /ˌgʊd'lʊkɪŋ/
grey *adj* /greɪ/
guest *n* /gest/
hair *n* /heə/
half *n* /hɑːf/
handsome *adj* /'hænsəm/
hat *n* /hæt/
hill *n* /hɪl/
jacket *n* /'dʒækɪt/
jumper *n* /'dʒʌmpə/
laugh *v* /lɑːf/
long *adj* /lɒŋ/
musician *n* /mjuː'zɪʃn/
pay *v* /peɪ/
pram *n* /præm/
rainbow *n* /'reɪnbəʊ/
roller skates *n pl* /'rəʊlə ˌskeɪts/
run *v* /rʌn/
shake (hands) *v* /ʃeɪk/
shiny *adj* /'ʃaɪni/
shirt *n* /ʃɜːt/
shoe *n* /ʃuː/
short *adj* /ʃɔːt/
shorts *n pl* /ʃɔːts/
silly *adj* /'sɪli/
size *n* /saɪz/
skateboard *n* /'skeɪtbɔːd/
skirt *n* /skɜːt/
sky *n* /skaɪ/
smile *v* /smaɪl/
smoke *v* /sməʊk/
sports car *n* /'spɔːts ˌkɑː/
starry *adj* /'stɑːri/
suit *n* /suːt/
sunglasses *n pl* /'sʌnglɑːsɪz/
T-shirt *n* /'tiː ʃɜːt/
talk *v* /tɔːk/
trainers *n pl* /'treɪnəz/
try on *v* /ˌtraɪ 'ɒn/
umbrella *n* /ʌm'brelə/
whose? *pron* /huːz/

Unit 12

accident *n* /'æksɪdənt/
adventure *n* /əd'ventʃə/
amazed *adj* /ə'meɪzd/
blouse *n* /blaʊz/
championship *n* /'tʃæmpiənʃɪp/
cloudy *adj* /'klaʊdi/
coast *n* /kəʊst/
cool *adj* /kuːl/
corner *n* /'kɔːnə/
degrees *n pl* /dɪ'griːz/
driving school *n* /'draɪvɪŋ ˌskuːl/
dry *adj* /draɪ/
excitement *n* /ɪk'saɪtmənt/
feel sick *v* /ˌfiːl 'sɪk/
float *v* /fləʊt/
foggy *adj* /'fɒgi/
forever *adv* /fɔː'revə/
forget *v* /fə'get/
fresh air *n* /ˌfreʃ 'eə/
full-time *adj* /ˌfʊl'taɪm/
garden shed *n* /ˌgɑːdn 'ʃed/
golf *n* /gɒlf/
grow up *v* /ˌgrəʊ 'ʌp/
lion *n* /'laɪən/
motor racing *n* /'məʊtə ˌreɪsɪŋ/
nervous *adj* /'nɜːvəs/
parachute *n* /'pærəʃuːt/
pyramid *n* /'pɪrəmɪd/
race *v* /reɪs/
racing circuit *n* /'reɪsɪŋ ˌsɜːkɪt/
racing driver *n* /'reɪsɪŋ ˌdraɪvə/
record *n* /'rekɔːd/
retire *v* /rɪ'taɪə/
safe *adj* /seɪf/
sky diving *n* /'skaɪ ˌdaɪvɪŋ/
sneeze *v* /sniːz/
star (TV) *n* /stɑː/
sunbathe *v* /'sʌnbeɪð/
swimming costume *n*
    /'swɪmɪŋ ˌkɒstjuːm/
top marks *n pl* /'tɒp 'mɑːks/
trouble *n* /'trʌbl/
tulip *n* /'tjuːlɪp/
view *n* /vjuː/
weather *n* /'weðə/
windsurfing *n* /'wɪndsɜːfɪŋ/
windy *adj* /'wɪndi/

Unit 13

annoyed *adj* /əˈnɔɪd/
arrive *v* /əˈraɪv/
badly *adv* /ˈbædli/
behave *v* /bɪˈheɪv/
behaviour *n* /bɪˈheɪvɪə/
burglar *n* /ˈbɜːglə/
carefully *adv* /ˈkeəfəli/
change (= money) *n* /tʃeɪndʒ/
depart *v* /dɪˈpɑːt/
elephant *n* /ˈelɪfənt/
explain *v* /ɪkˈspleɪn/
fast *adv* /fɑːst/
fluently *adv* /ˈfluːəntli/
fortunately *adv* /ˈfɔːtʃənətli/
generation *n* /ˌdʒenəˈreɪʃn/
gold medal *n* /ˈgəʊld ˈmedl/
grass *n* /grɑːs/
guitar *n* /gɪˈtɑː/
leather *n* /ˈleðə/
marathon *n* /ˈmærəθən/
migrate *v* /maɪˈgreɪt/
moon *n* /muːn/
pin *v* /pɪn/
platform *n* /ˈplætfɔːm/
please *v* /pliːz/
quietly *adv* /ˈkwaɪətli/
return ticket *n* /rɪˈtɜːn ˈtɪkɪt/
ridiculous *adj* /rɪˈdɪkjələs/
rude *adj* /ruːd/
sheep *n* /ʃiːp/
shout *v* /ʃaʊt/
slowly *adv* /ˈsləʊli/
station *n* /ˈsteɪʃn/
support (a team) *v* /səˈpɔːt/
tell a lie *v* /ˌtel ə ˈlaɪ/
timetable *n* /ˈtaɪmteɪbl/
typical *adj* /ˈtɪpɪkl/
untidy *adj* /ʌnˈtaɪdi/
weigh *v* /weɪ/
well-behaved *adj* /ˌwel bɪˈheɪvd/
whistle *v* /ˈwɪsl/
wolf *n* /wʊlf/
worrying *adj* /ˈwʌriɪŋ/

Unit 14

abroad *adv* /əˈbrɔːd/
airport *n* /ˈeəpɔːt/
ambulance driver *n*
    /ˈæmbjələns ˌdraɪvə/
announcement *n* /əˈnaʊnsmənt/
arrival hall *n* /əˈraɪvl ˌhɔːl/
board *v* /bɔːd/
boarding pass *n* /ˈbɔːdɪŋ ˌpɑːs/
boat ride *n* /ˈbəʊt ˌraɪd/
business class *n* /ˈbɪznəs ˌklɑːs/
call *n* /kɔːl/
certificate *n* /səˈtɪfɪkət/
check in *v* /ˌtʃek ˈɪn/
check-in desk *n* /ˈtʃek ɪn ˌdesk/
competition *n* /ˌkɒmpəˈtɪʃn/
crown *n* /kraʊn/
dawn *n* /dɔːn/
delay *v* /dɪˈleɪ/
delayed *pp* /dɪˈleɪd/
departures board *n*
    /dɪˈpɑːtʃəz ˌbɔːd/
departure lounge *n*
    /dɪˈpɑːtʃə ˌlaʊndʒ/
double-decker bus *n*
    /ˌdʌbl ˌdekə ˈbʌs/
dressmaker *n* /ˈdresmeɪkə/
engineer *n* /ˌendʒɪˈnɪə/
flag *n* /flæg/
flight *n* /flaɪt/
gate (in an airport) *n* /geɪt/
give up (= stop) *v* /ˌgɪv ˈʌp/
grandson *n* /ˈgrænˌsʌn/
Greece *n* /griːs/
heart attack *n* /ˈhɑːt əˌtæk/
honeymoon *n* /ˈhʌnimuːn/
horn (on a car) *n* /hɔːn/
Hungary *n* /ˈhʌŋgəri/
jewels *n pl* /ˈdʒuːəlz/
jumbo jet *n* /ˈdʒʌmbəʊ ˈdʒet/
jump *v* /dʒʌmp/
last call *n* /ˌlɑːst ˈkɔːl/
let (sb) down (= disappoint) *v*
    /ˌlet ˈdaʊn/
lottery *n* /ˈlɒtəri/
loud *adj* /laʊd/
luggage *n* /ˈlʌgɪdʒ/
lung cancer *n* /ˈlʌŋ ˌkænsə/
marmalade *n* /ˈmɑːməleɪd/
millionaire *n* /ˌmɪljəˈneə/
miss *v* /mɪs/
niece *n* /niːs/
now boarding /ˌnaʊ ˈbɔːdɪŋ/
pack (a bag) *v* /pæk/
passenger *n* /ˈpæsɪndʒə/
passport control
    /ˈpɑːspɔːt kənˈtrəʊl/
pipe (to smoke) *n* /paɪp/
pneumonia *n* /njuːˈməʊniə/
remind *v* /rɪˈmaɪnd/
rheumatic fever *n*
    /ruːˈmætɪk ˈfiːvə/

seat *n* /siːt/
secretary *n* /ˈsekrətri/
serious *adj* /ˈsɪəriəs/
suitcase *n* /ˈsuːtkeɪs/
tractor *n* /ˈtræktə/
trolley *n* /ˈtrɒli/

Appendix 1

IRREGULAR VERBS

Base form	Past Simple	Past Participle
be	was/were	been
become	became	become
begin	began	begun
break	broke	broken
bring	brought	brought
build	built	built
buy	bought	bought
can	could	been able
catch	caught	caught
choose	chose	chosen
come	came	come
cost	cost	cost
cut	cut	cut
do	did	done
drink	drank	drunk
drive	drove	driven
eat	ate	eaten
fall	fell	fallen
feel	felt	felt
fight	fought	fought
find	found	found
fly	flew	flown
forget	forgot	forgotten
get	got	got
give	gave	given
go	went	gone/been
grow	grew	grown
have	had	had
hear	heard	heard
hit	hit	hit
keep	kept	kept
know	knew	known
learn	learnt/learned	learnt/learned
leave	left	left
lose	lost	lost
make	made	made
meet	met	met
pay	paid	paid
put	put	put
read /ri:d/	read /red/	read /red/
ride	rode	ridden
run	ran	run
say	said	said
see	saw	seen
sell	sold	sold
send	sent	sent
shut	shut	shut
sing	sang	sung
sit	sat	sat
sleep	slept	slept
speak	spoke	spoken
spend	spent	spent
stand	stood	stood
steal	stole	stolen
swim	swam	swum
take	took	taken
tell	told	told
think	thought	thought
understand	understood	understood
wake	woke	woken
wear	wore	worn
win	won	won
write	wrote	written

Appendix 2

VERB PATTERNS

Verb + *-ing*	
like	
love	swimming
enjoy	
hate	cooking
finish	
stop	

Verb + *to* + infinitive	
choose	
decide	
forget	
promise	to go
need	
help	
hope	
try	to work
want	
would like	
would love	

Verb + *-ing* or *to* + infinitive	
begin	raining/to rain
start	

Modal auxiliary verbs	
can	
could	go
shall	
will	arrive
would	

Phonetic symbols

Consonants

1	/p/	as in	**pen** /pen/
2	/b/	as in	**big** /bɪg/
3	/t/	as in	**tea** /tiː/
4	/d/	as in	**do** /duː/
5	/k/	as in	**cat** /kæt/
6	/g/	as in	**go** /gəʊ/
7	/f/	as in	**four** /fɔː/
8	/v/	as in	**very** /'veri/
9	/s/	as in	**son** /sʌn/
10	/z/	as in	**zoo** /zuː/
11	/l/	as in	**live** /lɪv/
12	/m/	as in	**my** /maɪ/
13	/n/	as in	**near** /nɪə/
14	/h/	as in	**happy** /'hæpi/
15	/r/	as in	**red** /red/
16	/j/	as in	**yes** /jes/
17	/w/	as in	**want** /wɒnt/
18	/θ/	as in	**thanks** /θæŋks/
19	/ð/	as in	**the** /ðə/
20	/ʃ/	as in	**she** /ʃiː/
21	/ʒ/	as in	**television** /'telɪvɪʒn/
22	/tʃ/	as in	**child** /tʃaɪld/
23	/dʒ/	as in	**German** /'dʒɜːmən/
24	/ŋ/	as in	**English** /'ɪŋglɪʃ/

Vowels

25	/iː/	as in	**see** /siː/
26	/ɪ/	as in	**his** /hɪz/
27	/i/	as in	**twenty** /'twenti/
28	/e/	as in	**ten** /ten/
29	/æ/	as in	**stamp** /stæmp/
30	/ɑː/	as in	**father** /'fɑːðə/
31	/ɒ/	as in	**hot** /hɒt/
32	/ɔː/	as in	**morning** /'mɔːnɪŋ/
33	/ʊ/	as in	**football** /'fʊtbɔːl/
34	/uː/	as in	**you** /juː/
35	/ʌ/	as in	**sun** /sʌn/
36	/ɜː/	as in	**learn** /lɜːn/
37	/ə/	as in	**letter** /'letə/

Diphthongs (two vowels together)

38	/eɪ/	as in	**name** /neɪm/
39	/əʊ/	as in	**no** /nəʊ/
40	/aɪ/	as in	**my** /maɪ/
41	/aʊ/	as in	**how** /haʊ/
42	/ɔɪ/	as in	**boy** /bɔɪ/
43	/ɪə/	as in	**hear** /hɪə/
44	/eə/	as in	**where** /weə/
45	/ʊə/	as in	**tour** /tʊə/

OXFORD
UNIVERSITY PRESS

Great Clarendon Street, Oxford OX2 6DP

Oxford University Press is a department of the University of Oxford. It furthers the University's objective of excellence in research, scholarship, and education by publishing worldwide in

Oxford New York

Auckland Cape Town Dar es Salaam Hong Kong Karachi Kuala Lumpur Madrid Melbourne Mexico City Nairobi New Delhi Shanghai Taipei Toronto

With offices in

Argentina Austria Brazil Chile Czech Republic France Greece Guatemala Hungary Italy Japan South Korea Poland Portugal Singapore Switzerland Thailand Turkey Ukraine Vietnam

OXFORD and OXFORD ENGLISH are registered trade marks of Oxford University Press in the UK and in certain other countries

© Oxford University Press 2004

The moral rights of the author have been asserted

Database right Oxford University Press (maker)

First published 2000

2009 2008 2007 2006 2005
20 19 18 17 16 15

ISBN-13: 978 0 19 436677 9 INTERNATIONAL EDITION
ISBN-10: 0-19-436677-4
ISBN-13: 978 0 19 437875 8 GERMAN EDITION
ISBN-10: 0-19-437875-6
BESTELLNUMMER 118 258

Printed in China

ACKNOWLEDGEMENTS

The authors and publisher are grateful to those who have given permission to reproduce the following extracts and adaptations of copyright material: p24 'It's a job for nine men, but someone's got to do it' by Rebecca Fowler. *The Mail Night* and *Day Magazine* 3 May 1998. © The *Mail on Sunday.*

p40 'The jet settler' by Andy Lines. *The Mirror, Cover Magazine* March 1999. © Mirror Group Newspapers.

p48 'Refugee's daughter hailed as new Picasso' by Nigel Reynolds. *The Daily Telegraph* 12 March 1996. © Telegraph Group Ltd.

p48 'Shy 10-year-old piano prodigy' by David Ward. *The Guardian* 23 September 1997. © The Guardian.

p87 'What a wonderful world'. Words and Music by George David Weiss and George Douglas © 1967 Range Road Music, Inc., Quartet Music, Inc. and Abilene Music, Inc., USA. – Copyright Renewed – All Rights Reserved. 50% Lyric reproduction by kind permission of Carlin Music Corporation, 50% by kind permission of Memory Lane Music Limited.

p102 'The Story-Teller' from Tooth and Claw (Oxford Bookworms Series) by Rosemary Border.

p110 'Discover the secrets of a long life' by Katy Macdonald. *The Daily Mail* 2 November 1993. © The *Daily Mail.*

p112 'Leaving on a jet plane' by John Denver © 1967, Cherry Lane Music Limited, c/o Harmony Music Limited, 11 Uxbridge Street, London W8 7TQ.

Every endeavour has been made to identify the sources of all material used. The publisher apologises for any omissions.

Illustrations by: Kathy Baxendale pp17, 96; Rowie Christopher pp45, 86–87, 98–99; Martin Cottam pp103, 104; Neil Gower pp43, 81; Jane Hadfield p66; John Holder pp102–3, 104; Sarah Jones pp11, 65; Ian Kellas pp31, 32, 44, 69, 76, 84–5, 92, 97, 100; Andy Parker p84; Pierre Paul Pariseau pp96–7; Debbie Ryder p80; Colin Salmon p40; Harry Venning pp6, 16, 34, 39, 62, 77, 81, 85, 88, 98, 99, 101

The publishers would like to thank the following for their kind permission to reproduce photographs: AKG Photos pp47 (Mozart), 62 (Levi Strauss), 79 (Eric Lessing/Vienna Operahouse); *Associated Press* pp42 (Susan Sterner/beach), 59 (Big Ben), 74; *Barnabys Picture Library* pp20 (doctor), 26 (nurse), 32 (autumn), 108 (Stuart D Hall/Brad & Marilyn); *Bayer* p62 (Hoffman & Aspirin bottle), *John Birdsill Photography* pp12, 51 (black woman on phone), 82 (Nadia & Rudi), 83 (Flora & Toni); *Catherine Blackie* p110 (Tommy young, Joyce young and old); *Anthony Blake Photo Library* pp26 (John Sims/barman), 71 (John Sims/bananas), 72 (Sian Irving/pasta, Andrew Sydenham/chocolate cakes, Gerrit Buntrock/bacon & eggs); *Bridgeman Art Library* pp56 (The Hall of Representatives/The Signing of the Constitution of the United States in 1787, 1940 by Howard Chandler Christy), 57 (Pennsylvania Academy of Fine Arts, Philadelphia/George Washington at Princeton by Charles Willson Peale 1741–1827), 79 (Coram Foundation/Handel's Messiah); *Camera Press* pp55 (Mark Stewart/ flowers), 56 (M Thatcher & family, Jon Blau/M Thatcher at conference), 61 (cars); *Collections* pp26 (Brian Shuel/shopkeeper, Nick Oakes/architect), 110 (old Tommy), 111 (Anthea Sieveking/Alice old); *Corbis Images* p47 (Einstein), 53 (cotton picking), 62 (JL Baird); *Corbis Sygma* pp26 (Mathiew/Journalist), 55 (R Ellis/Clinton & Blair), 57 (M Polak/M Thatcher resignation), 82 (Ruth, Cathy & Jane; *Zoe Dominic* p47 (Nureyev); *European Commission* p26 (interpreter); *Format Photographers* pp11 (Joanne O'Brien/Leo), 83 (Ulrike Preuss/Becca); *Greg Evans International* pp42 (Greg Balfour Evans/Alise), 58 (Greg Balfour Evans/Easter Eggs), 112 (Greg Balfour Evans/plane; *Food Features* p72 (Indian curry); *Getty One Stone* pp7 (John Riley/Max & Lisa), 16–17 (Joseph Pobereskin/Central Park), 25 (David Tomlinson), 32 (Manuela, Chad Ehlers/beach), 33 (Bruce Ayres/Toshi, cherry blossom, Rich Iwasaki/ maple trees), 42 (Dennis McColeman/Toronto), 33 (P Crowther & S Carter/Euro Symbol), 58 (Bob Thomas/ wedding), 58 (Bruce Ayres/Thanksgiving, James Randklev/Christmas tree), p59 (Andrew Olney/girl & cake), 64 (Phil Schofield/fisherman, Martin Rogers/ man & laptop, Walter Hodges/girl on computer, Michelangelo Gratton/girl on beach), 64–5 (Mark Andrew/message in bottle), 71 (Wayne astep/Shammar tribe eating, Yann Lavma/China woman & child, David Baird/strawberry crates), 72 (Martin Barraud/Sally), 73 (Timothy Shonnard)

(ferry), 83 (Ian O'Leary/businessman), 86–7 (baby), 93 (Suzanne & Nick Geary/tulips), 93 (safari, Donald Nausbaum/Copacabana Beach, John Lamb/Red Square), 108 (Paul Figura/Ryan); *Sue Glass* p95 (Sue Glass racing & portrait); *The Guardian* p48–9 (Don McPhee/Lukas Vondracek); *Robert Harding Picture Library* pp8 (P Bouchon/Maria), 26 (pilot, Ken Gilham/postman), 32 (Norma Joseph/Al Wheeler), 42 (J Lightfoot/Lisbon, Int Stock/Ray & Elsie), 51 (teenager on phone), 54 (Bob Jacobson/Simon), 59 (Mark Mawson/pumpkin), 72 (Rex Rouchon/Lucy), 76 (Norma Joseph/Plaza), 83 (Tony Demi/Angela, David Hughes/Juan), 93 (pyramids, Taj Mahal); *Hulton Getty Picture Collection* pp47 (Picasso), 52 (Cotton picking), 56 (G. W. as farmer), 60 (jeans), 61 (phone calls, television); *Image Bank* pp8 (Juan Silva/Lena & Miguel), 11 (Stephen Derr/ Mary), 61 (Archive Photos/ hamburgers); *Impact Photos* pp21 (Andy Johnstone/ barman), 51 (Giles Barnard/female bank worker), 59 (Simon Shepherd/Valentines Day); *Insight* pp24–25; *Katz* p60 (Mansell/planes), 71 (Benoit Decout/ restaurants Lyon); *Sally Lack* p111 (Alice); *The Mandarin Hotel* p76; *Network Photographers* pp8 (Pierre), 20 (Peter Jordan/Scientist), 51 (Homer Sykes/man on phone); *Pictures* p72 (Chinese food); *Popperfoto* pp15 (M.C.C./family at dinner table), 55 (Bob Thomas/World Cup), 60 (Coca Cola, records, photograph), 61 (bikes); *Clem Quinn* p95 (Clem Quinn skydiving & portrait); *Quadrant Picture Library* p113; *Redferns* pp78 (David Redfern), 86; *Henry Reichhold* pp108–9; *Rex Features* pp40–1, 48–9 (Di Crollalanza/Alexandra Nechita); *The Savoy Group* p76 (Claridges); *The Stock Market* pp8 (Anna), 75, 93 (K Owaki/canyon and Mt Fuji), 93 (Great Wall, dancer), 94 (skydivers); *Telegraph Colour Library* pp11 (Benelux Press/Flora), 52 (Colorific/woman on verandah); *Topham Picturepoint* pp71 (Japanese restaurant), 79 (Beatles); *Trip Photo Library* pp7 (E James/Rafael, M Fairman/Tomoko), 8 (B North/Yasima, D Morgan/Irina, A Tovy/Lázló & Ilona), 9 (E James), 11 (M Stevenson/ Edward), 15 (Japanese family, S Grant/Mixed race family, B Seed/ Portugese family), 22, 23, 26 (S Grant/accountant), 39 (P Treanor/Pierre), 42 (D Cole/Samoan house, Mike Clement/Manola, N Menneer/Brad), 45 (H Rogers/ Tina), 51 (H Rogers/woman in T shirt), 51 (Grant/ man in office), 70 (H Rogers/S. Indian children), 71 (F Good/rice harvest, H Rogers/ship), 72 (Andrews/Gavin. H Rogers/Graham and Lucy)

Commissioned photography by: Gareth Boden: pp6, 7 (school), 8 (Richard/Kurt), 11 (Bianca)35, 67 (school dinners), 75; *Haddon Davies:* pp37, 67 (biscuits), 89, 105; *Mark Mason:* pp10, 18, 27, 68; *Maggie Milner:* pp14, 19, 46; *Stephen Ogilvy:* p17

We would like to thank the following for their assistance: Bell Language School, British Telecom plc, Gabucci, Leventhorpe School, Photosound